ANATOMY & PHYSIOLOGY Coloring Book

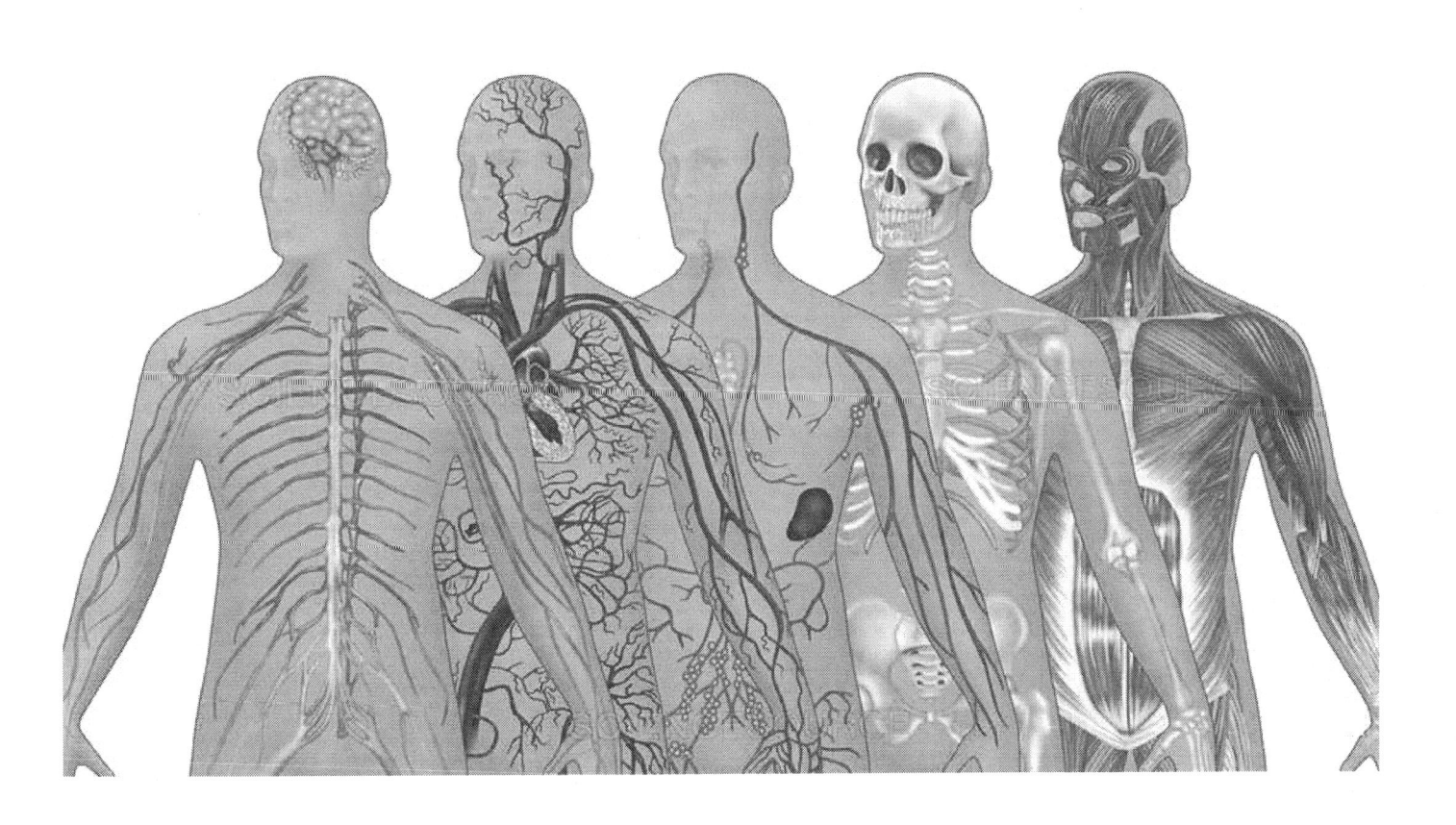

For kids & teens

**FROM
DS PUBLICATION INC.**

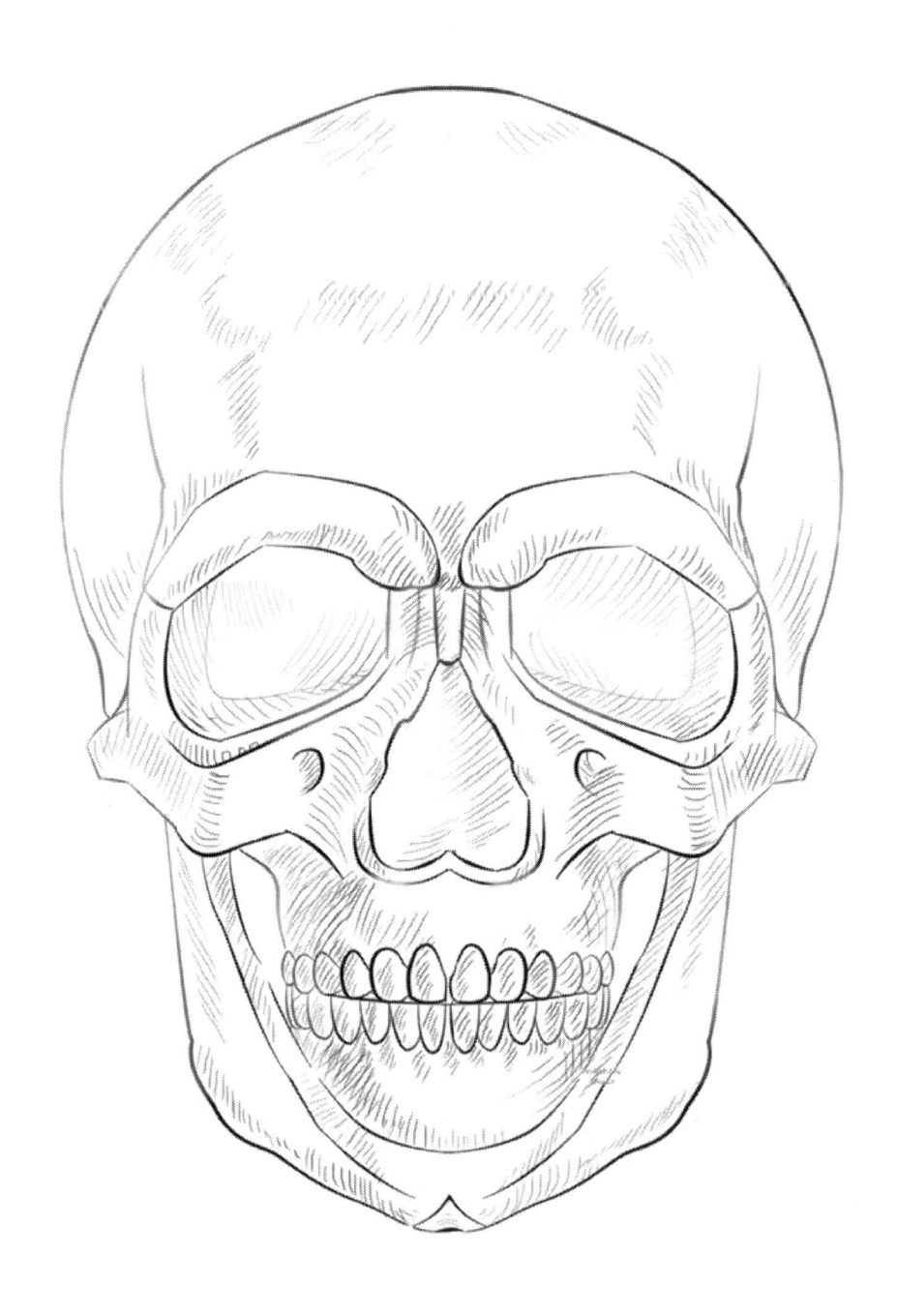

Please leave a review after using this book. If there is any error, It will help us to rectify the errors and also helps to create quality books. All right reserved to the respective owner.

*Note: some of the sketches rotated left due to its large size of the sketches.
©Dhanraj Subbiah

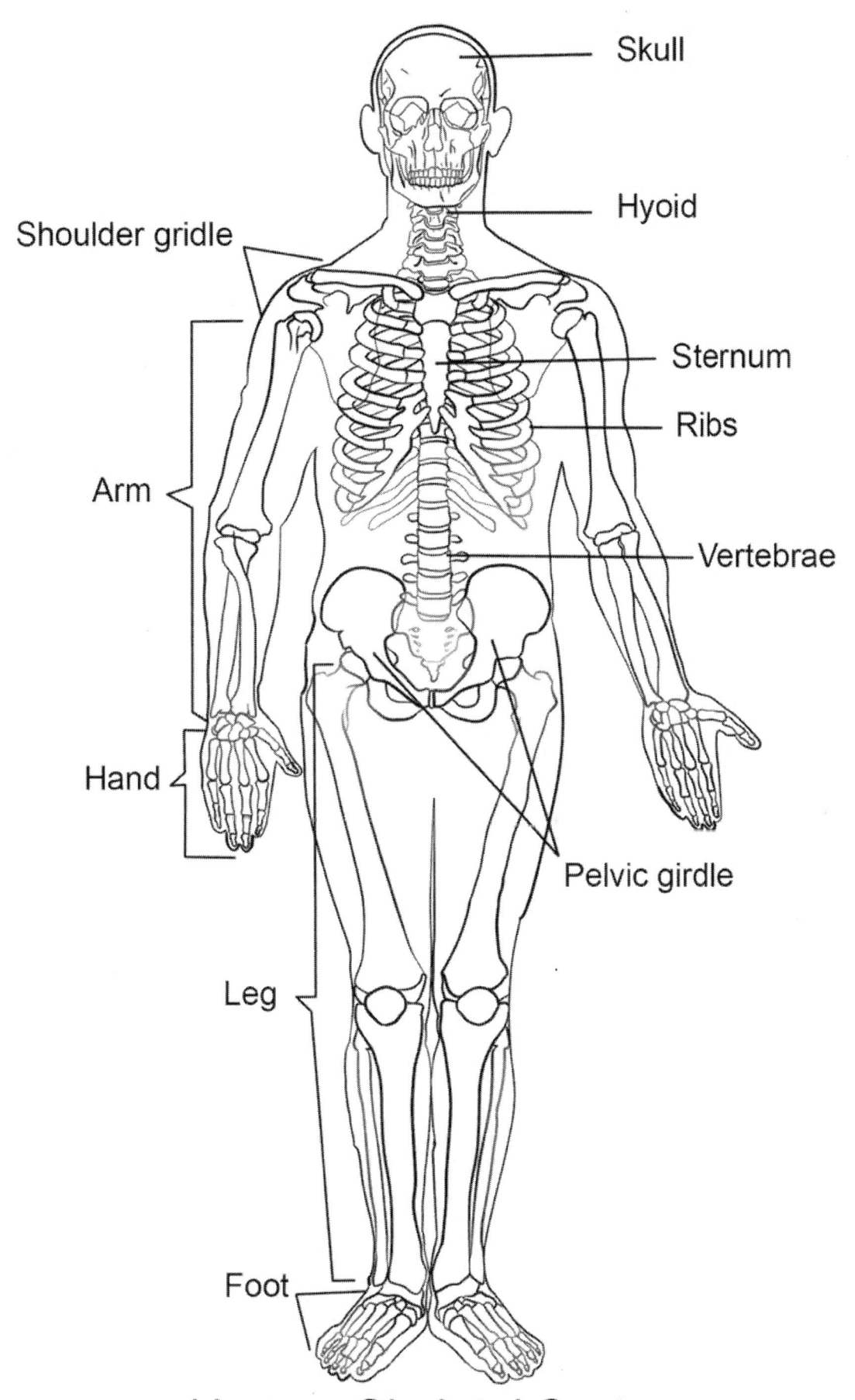

Human Skeletal System

- Skull
- Hyoid
- Shoulder gridle
- Sternum
- Ribs
- Arm
- Vertebrae
- Hand
- Pelvic girdle
- Leg
- Foot

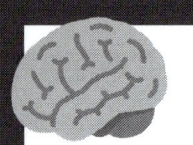

Circulatory systems

Circulatory System

The circulatory system consists of the heart and blood vessels which encompass all of the arteries, veins, and capillaries. The arteries carry oxygenated blood away from the heart, and veins return deoxygenated blood back to the heart. The main purpose of the circulatory system is to transport blood, oxygen, nutrients, and hormones to and from different cells and tissues throughout the body. This system works hand-in-hand with the respiratory system to facilitate the exchange of oxygen and carbon dioxide within the blood per the alveoli in the lungs. It is also very important for the removal of wastes and poisons within the body via the digestive and urinary systems.

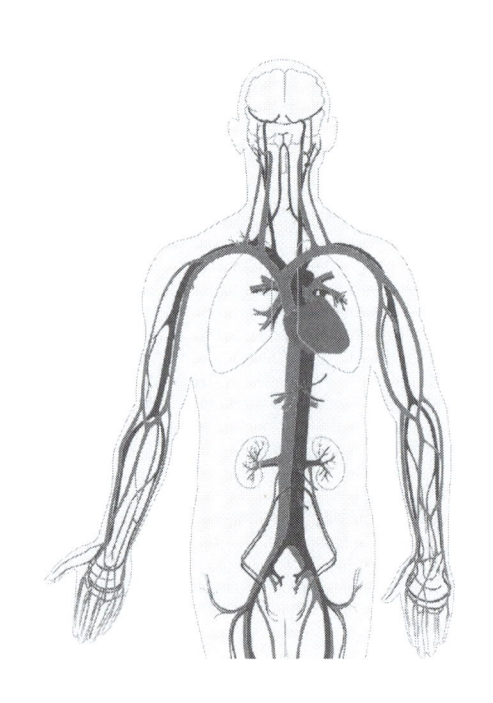

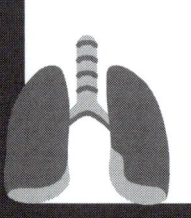

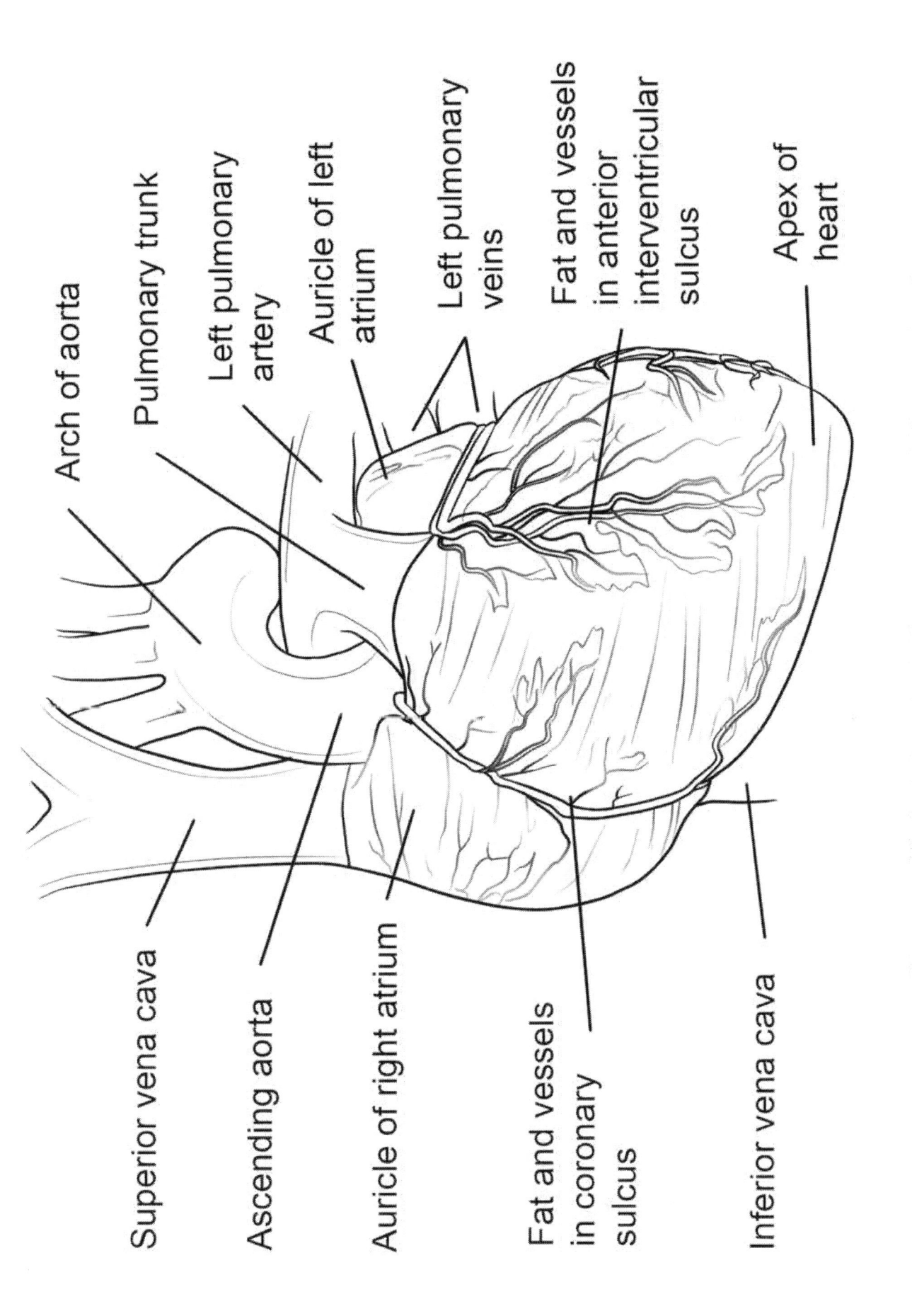

Superficial Heart Anatomy (Anterior)

- Arch of aorta
- Pulmonary trunk
- Left pulmonary artery
- Auricle of left atrium
- Left pulmonary veins
- Fat and vessels in anterior interventricular sulcus
- Apex of heart
- Superior vena cava
- Ascending aorta
- Auricle of right atrium
- Fat and vessels in coronary sulcus
- Inferior vena cava

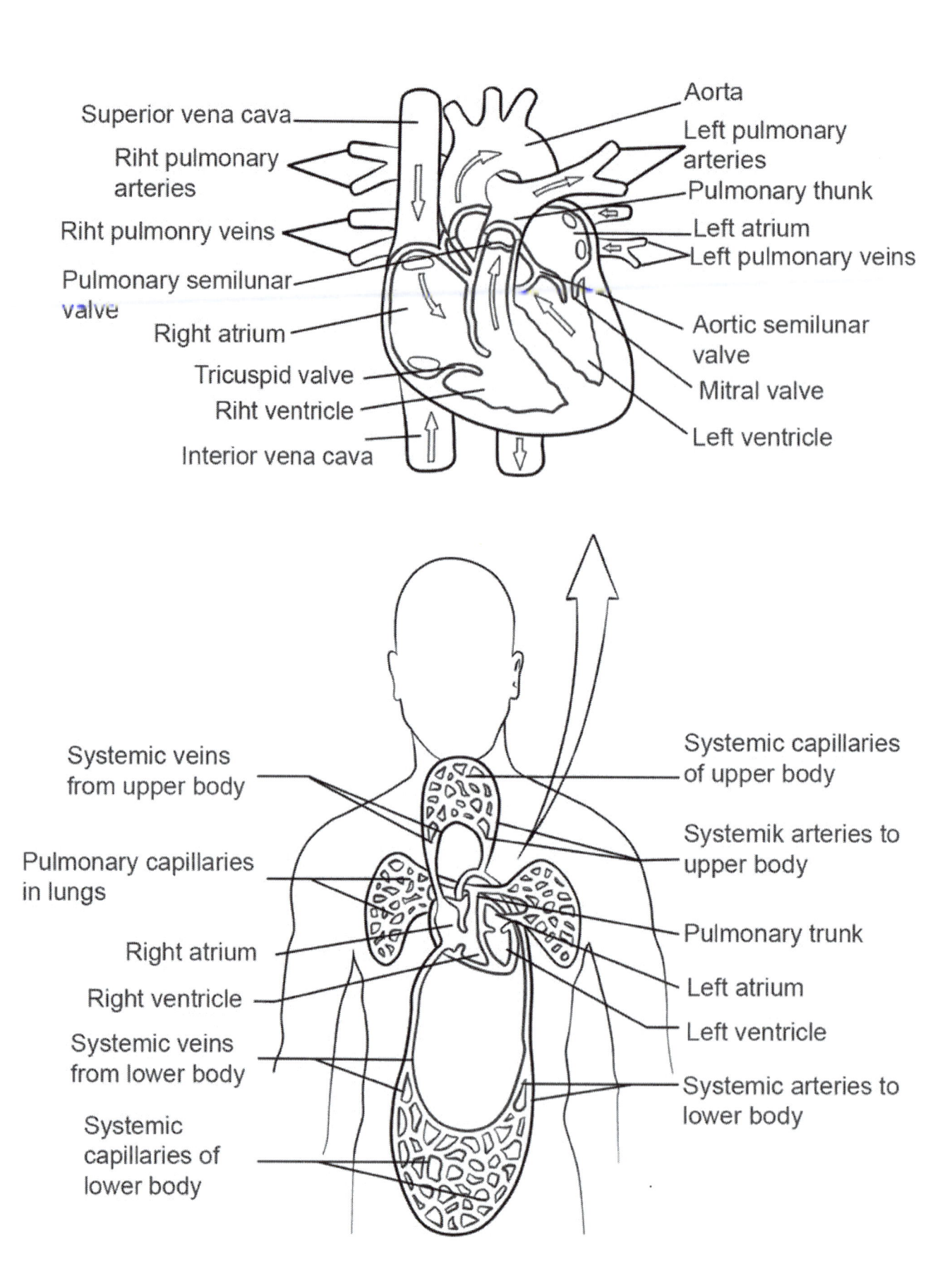

Superior vena cava
Riht pulmonary arteries
Riht pulmonry veins
Pulmonary semilunar valve
Right atrium
Tricuspid valve
Riht ventricle
Interior vena cava

Aorta
Left pulmonary arteries
Pulmonary thunk
Left atrium
Left pulmonary veins
Aortic semilunar valve
Mitral valve
Left ventricle

Systemic veins from upper body
Pulmonary capillaries in lungs
Right atrium
Right ventricle
Systemic veins from lower body
Systemic capillaries of lower body

Systemic capillaries of upper body
Systemik arteries to upper body
Pulmonary trunk
Left atrium
Left ventricle
Systemic arteries to lower body

Human Circulatory System

Respiratory systems

The respiratory system primarily consists of the trachea, bronchi, bronchioles, alveoli, lungs, and diaphragm. Its primary functions are to absorb oxygen through the inhalation (inspiration) of air and to expel carbon dioxide back out into the atmosphere through exhalation (expiration). This process is commonly called ventilation, otherwise known as breathing, which facilitates the exchange of oxygen and carbon dioxide between the lungs and atmosphere. Within the lungs, oxygen and carbon dioxide are exchanged via the alveoli, which are tiny air sacs where this action takes place. During this process, the newly oxygenated blood is pumped through the circulatory system by way of the heart to all of the cells, tissues, and organs throughout the body.

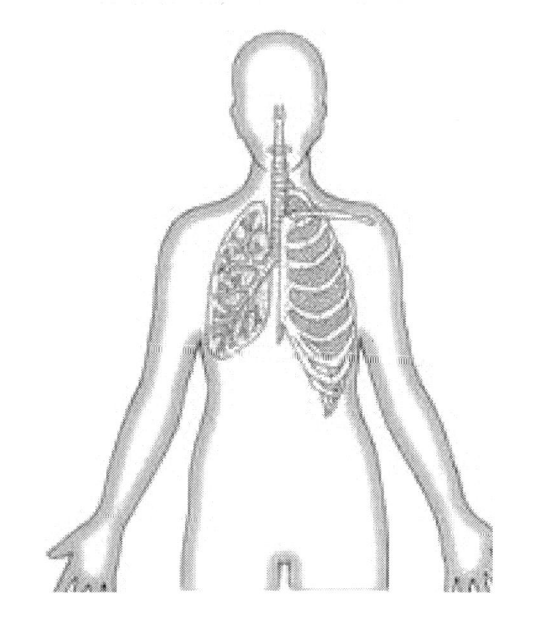

The Respiratory System

- Frontal sinus
- Nasal conchae
- Nose
- Larynx
- Trachea
- Bronchus
- Bronchioles
- Left lung
- Sphenoidal sinus
- Nasal cavity
- Pharynx
- Alveoli
- Right lung
- Diaphragm

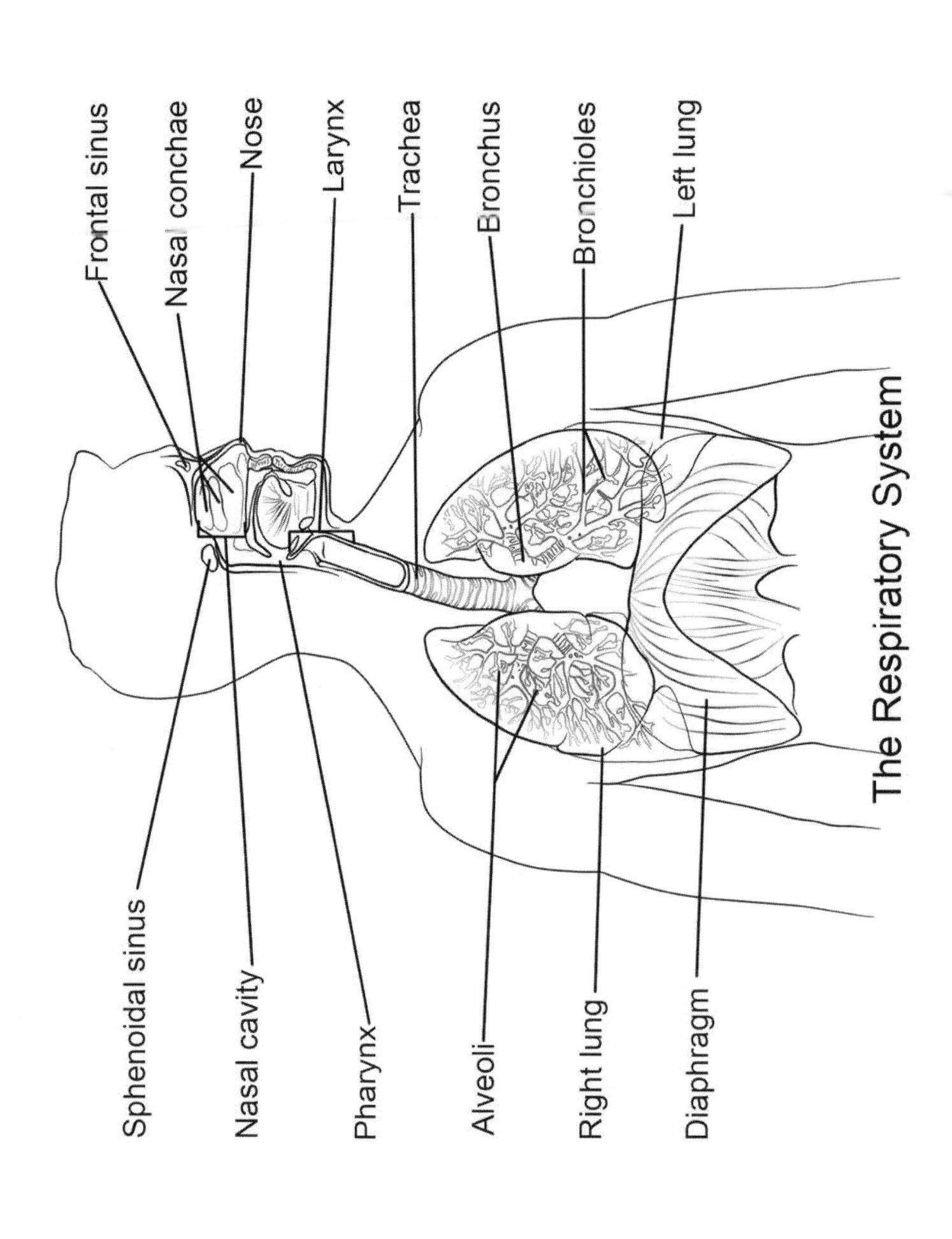

Anatomy of the Human Lung

- Trachea
- Superior lobe
- Main (primary) bronchus
- Lobal (secondary) bronchus
- Segmental (tertiary) bronchus
- Cardiac notch
- Inferior lobe
- Left lung
- Right lung
- Superior lobe
- Middle lobe
- Inferior lobe

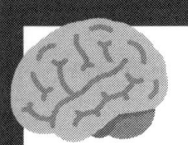

Endocrine systems

The endocrine system is primarily made up of the hypothalamus, thyroid, parathyroid, pituitary, pineal body, adrenal glands, pancreas, and reproductive glands. The main function of this system is to help regulate and maintain assorted functions of the body by releasing hormones into the bloodstream to maintain homeostasis. Homeostasis is the condition of maintaining balance within the body in relation to its external environment and is vital for life. Hormones are chemical substances produced by a gland, or glands, to affect other parts of the body. Together these glands are responsible for growth and development, breathing and heart rate, reproduction, metabolism, mood, sleep, tissue function, digestion, the release of insulin, and much more.

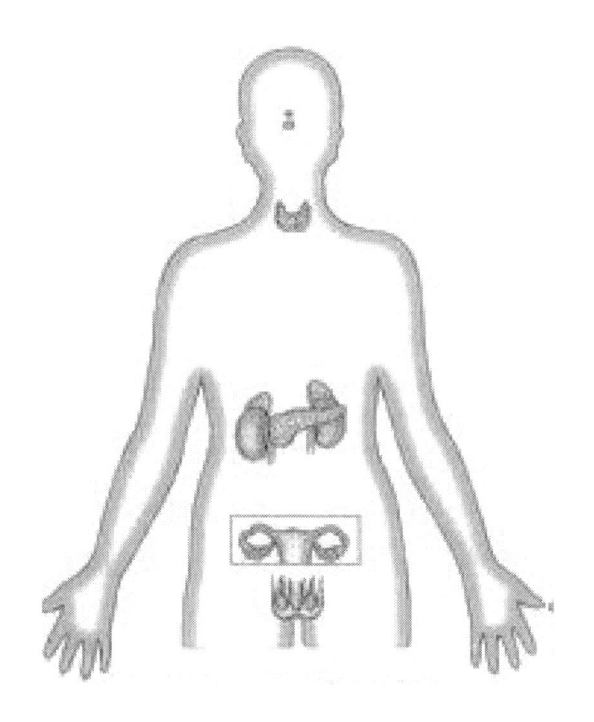

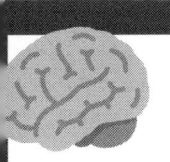

Digestive systems

The digestive system consists mainly of the gastrointestinal (digestive) tract which includes the mouth, esophagus, stomach, small intestine, and large intestine (colon). The liver, gallbladder, and pancreas are also a part of this system and are responsible for contributing to the chemical breakdown of ingested food. The main functions of the digestive system are digestion, absorption, and the elimination of waste. Digestion is the breakdown of foods by mechanical and enzymatic processes into substances that can be utilized by the body. Absorption occurs primarily in the small intestine and is the process by which vitamins, minerals, carbohydrates, fats, and proteins are passed on to the blood for energy. Undigested and non-useful nutrients from food pass through to the large intestine and are eliminated as waste. The large intestine is also where the majority of water and sodium is absorbed into the body for use.

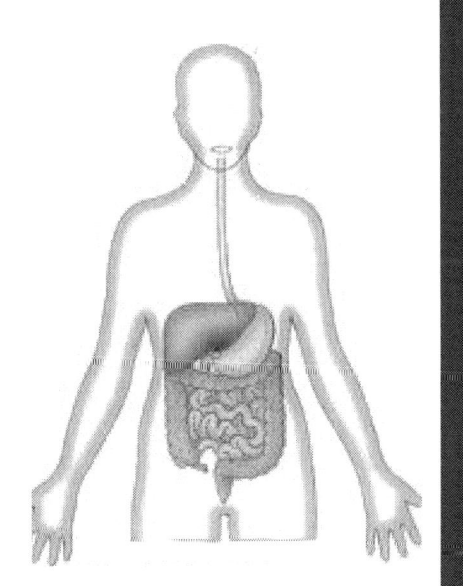

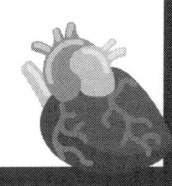

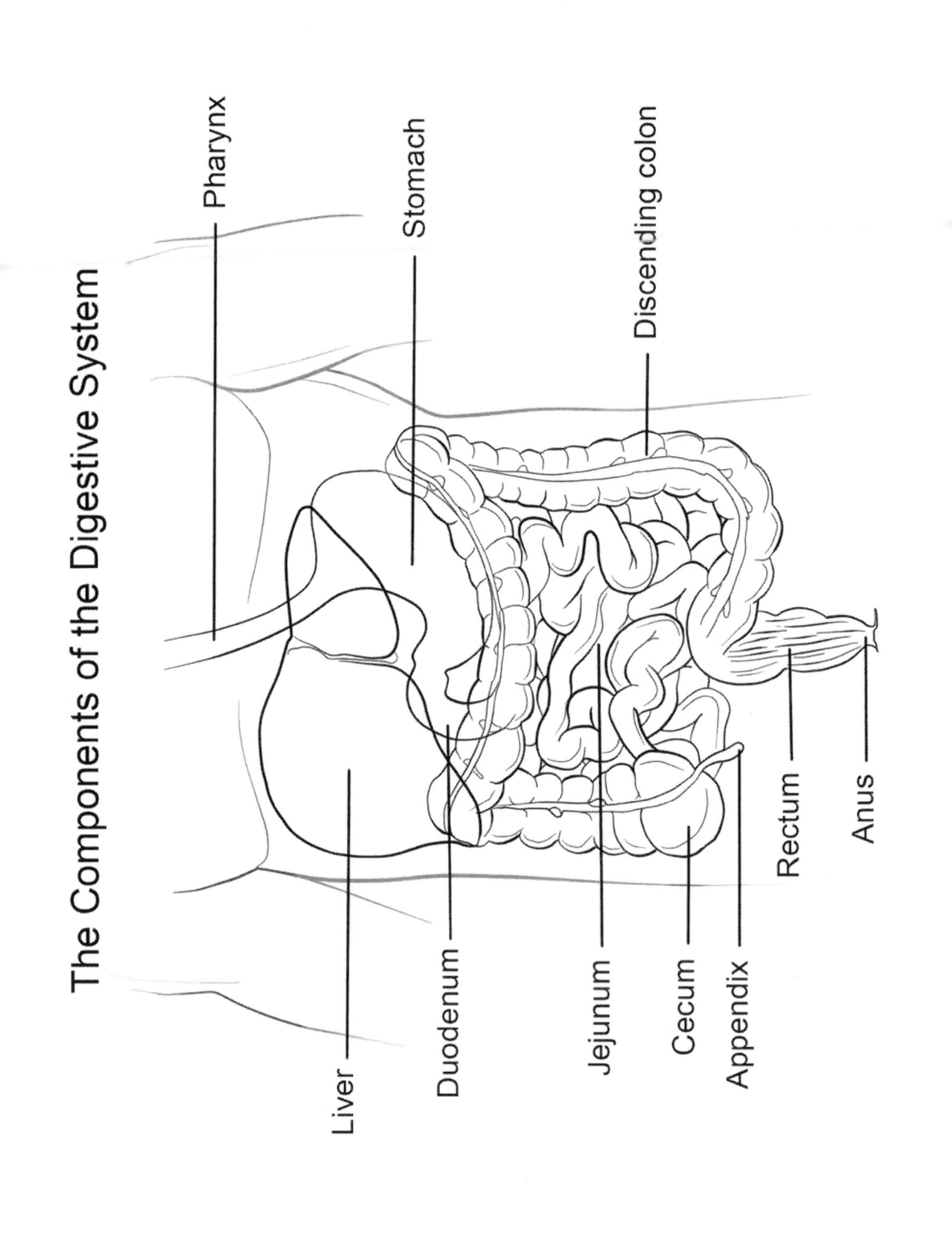

The Components of the Digestive System

- Pharynx
- Stomach
- Discending colon
- Liver
- Duodenum
- Jejunum
- Cecum
- Appendix
- Rectum
- Anus

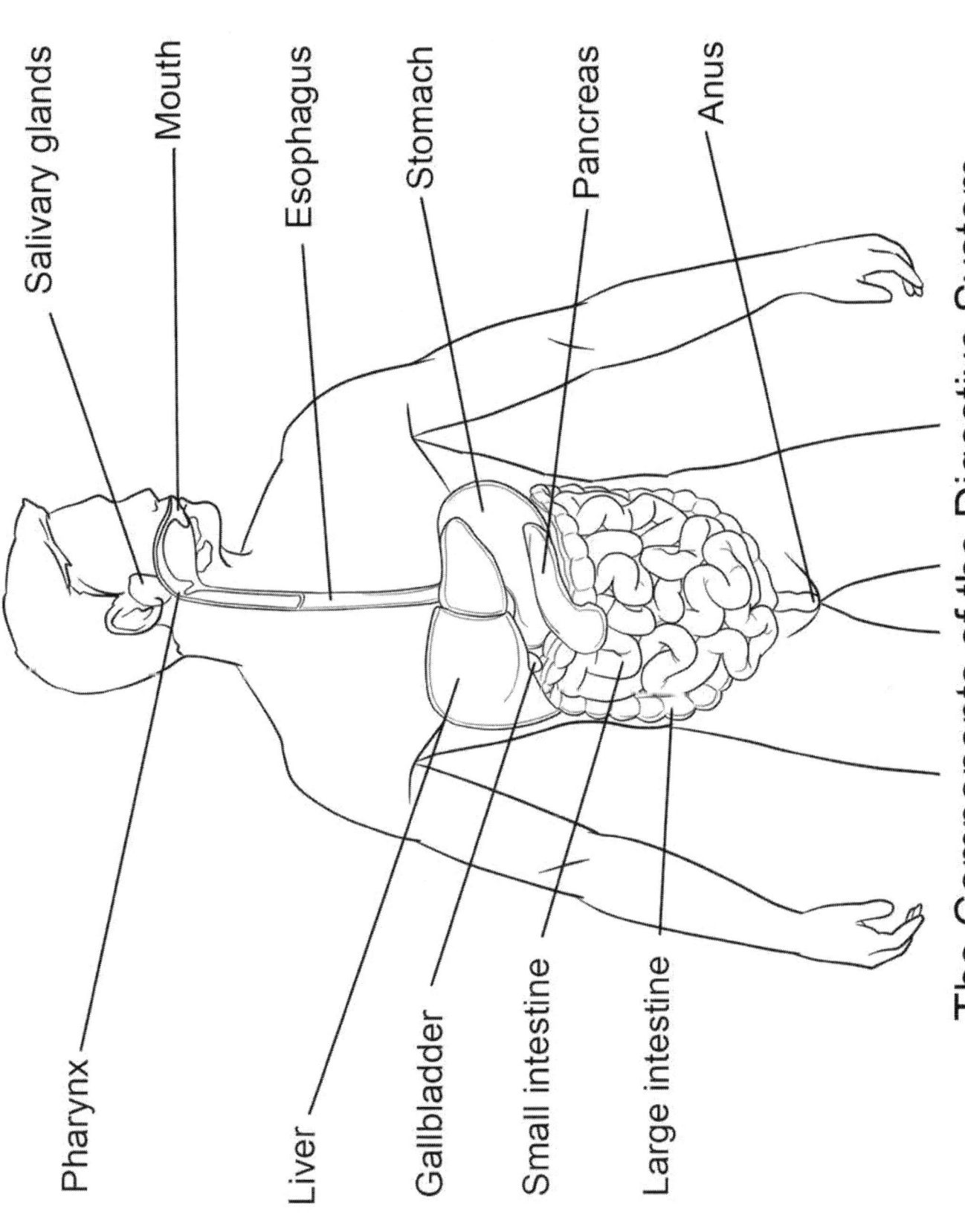

The Components of the Digestive System

- Salivary glands
- Mouth
- Pharynx
- Esophagus
- Stomach
- Liver
- Gallbladder
- Pancreas
- Small intestine
- Large intestine
- Anus

Human Stomach

- Esophagus
- Cardial noth
- Fundus
- Cardia
- Body
- Angular incisure
- Pyloric canal
- Pylorus
- Pyloric antrum
- Duodenum

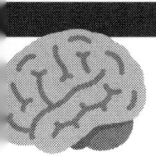

Nervous systems

The nervous system is made up of two major parts: the central nervous system (CNS) and the peripheral nervous system (PNS). The central nervous system is made up of the brain and spinal cord and acts as the main control system for the body. The peripheral nervous system is made up of all the nerves and ganglia (nerve cell clusters) found outside of the central nervous system; its role is receiving information from various stimuli and sending it to the brain. The main purpose of the nervous system is perceiving information from inside the body and/or from the external environment (PNS) and determining how the body responds to any changes (CNS). An example of this would be pricking your finger on a needle, your body will immediately pull your finger away in direct response to painful stimuli. This system also regulates basic bodily functions such as breathing, blood pressure, digestion, and the control of body temperature.

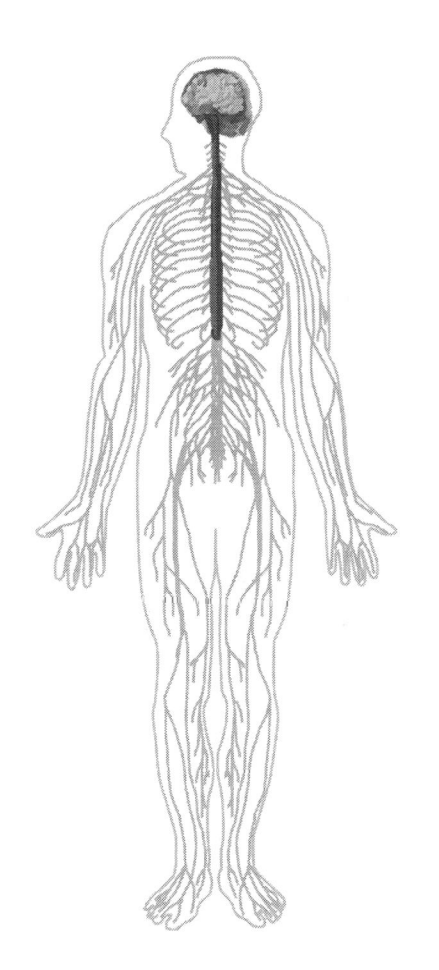

Central Nervous System

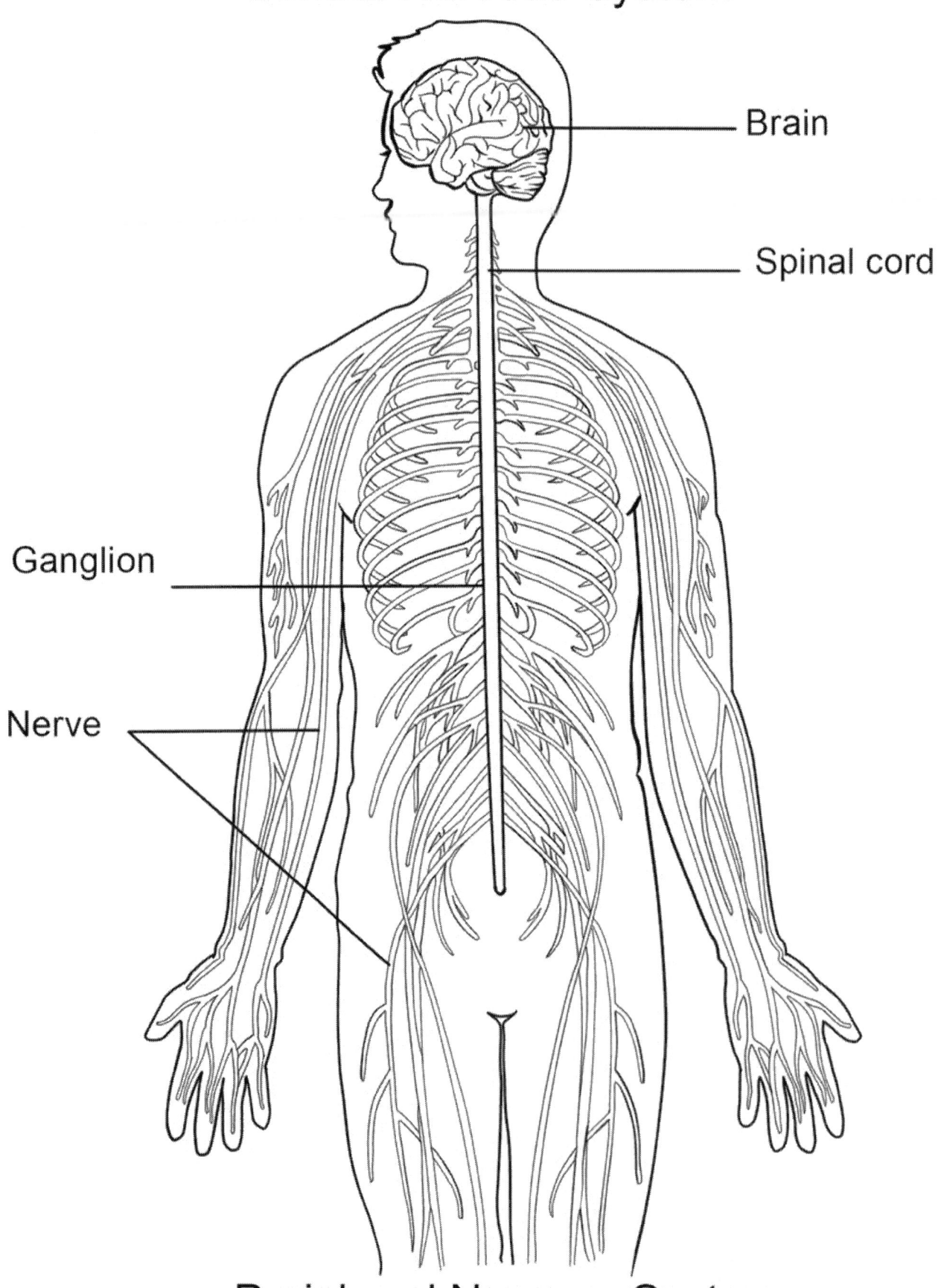

- Brain
- Spinal cord
- Ganglion
- Nerve

Peripheral Nervous System

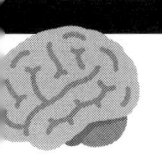

Muscular systems

The muscular system consists of 650 skeletal, smooth (visceral), and cardiac (myocardium) muscles. The primary functions of this system are movement, joint stabilization, heat generation, maintenance of posture, and the facilitation of blood circulation. Skeletal muscles connect to the bone and work hand-in-hand with the skeletal system to control voluntary movement such as walking and running. Smooth muscles are involuntary muscles that are responsible for the contraction of hollow muscles which include the stomach, intestines, bladder, and uterus. Cardiac muscle is an involuntary muscle found only in the heart and facilitates the circulation of blood by pumping it to the major arteries and out into the body via the circulatory

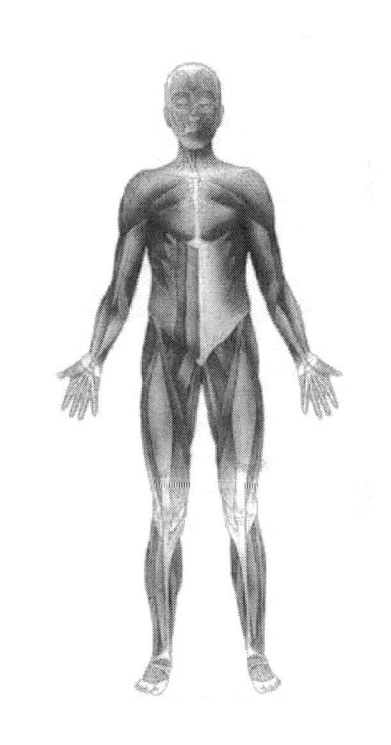

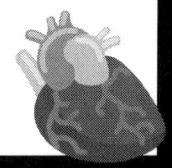

Trapezius

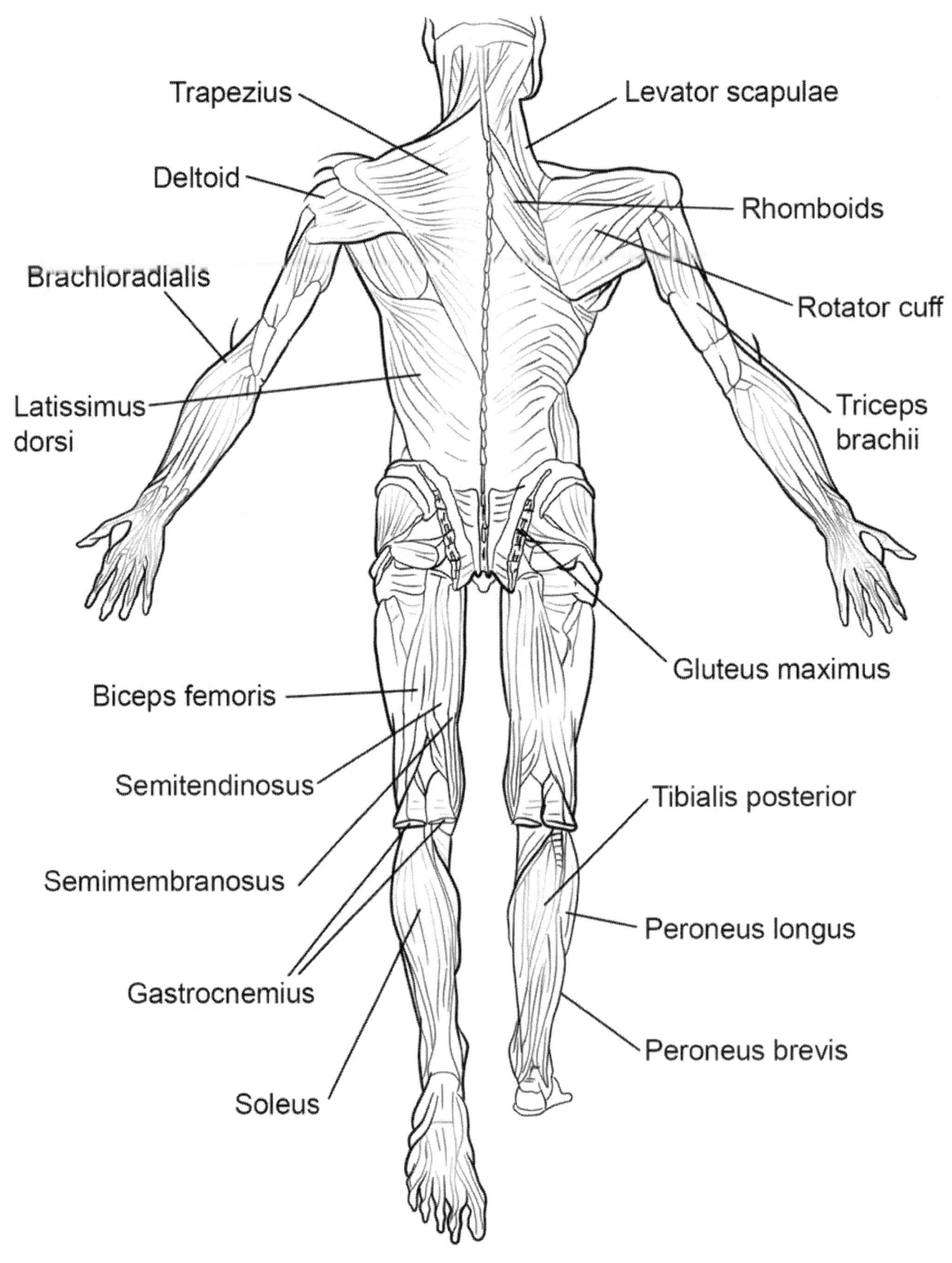

Levator scapulae

Deltoid

Rhomboids

Brachloradlalis

Rotator cuff

Latissimus dorsi

Triceps brachii

Gluteus maximus

Biceps femoris

Semitendinosus

Tibialis posterior

Semimembranosus

Peroneus longus

Gastrocnemius

Peroneus brevis

Soleus

Human Muscles

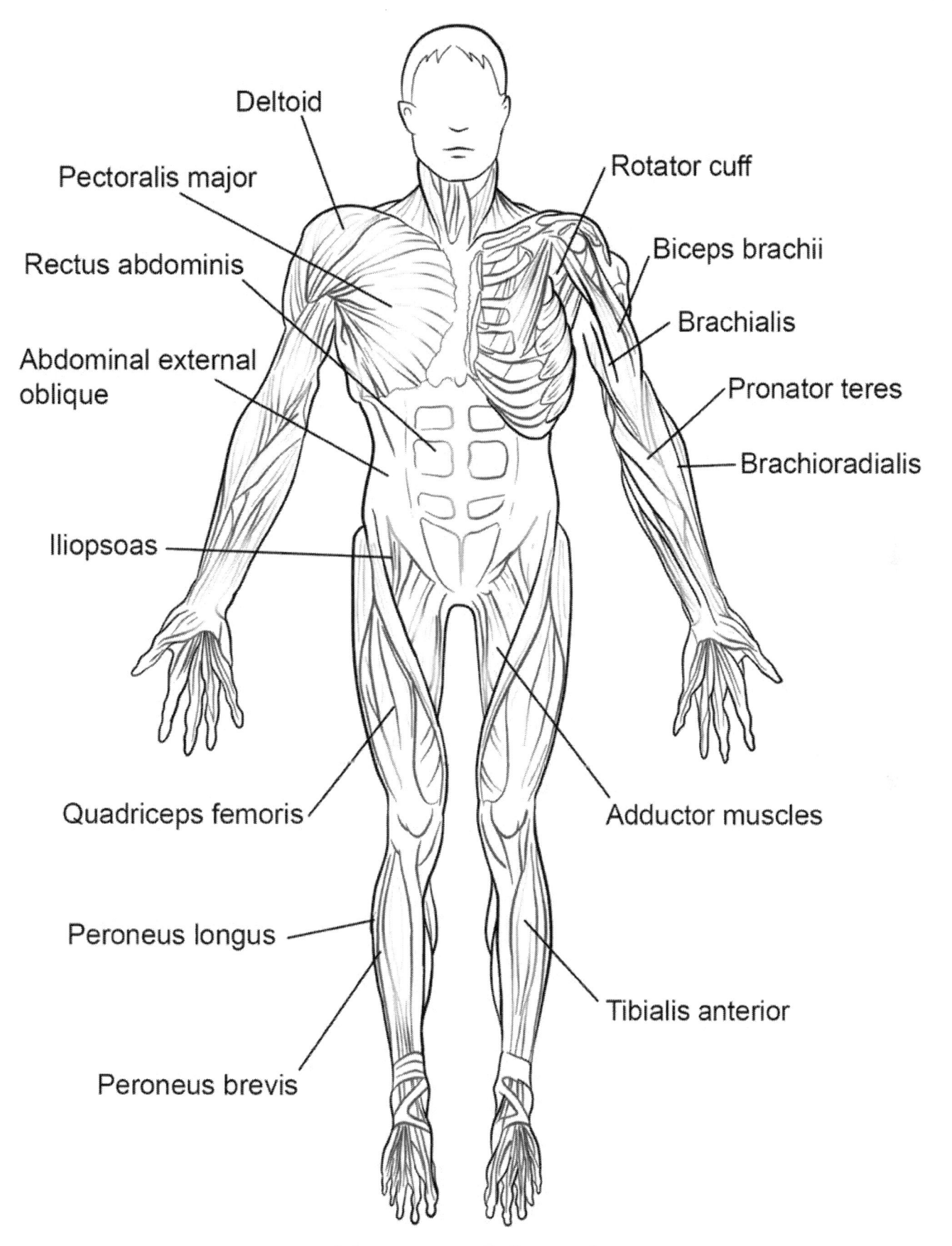

Human Muscles

- Deltoid
- Pectoralis major
- Rectus abdominis
- Abdominal external oblique
- Iliopsoas
- Quadriceps femoris
- Peroneus longus
- Peroneus brevis
- Rotator cuff
- Biceps brachii
- Brachialis
- Pronator teres
- Brachioradialis
- Adductor muscles
- Tibialis anterior

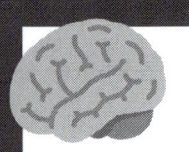

Lymphatic systems

The lymphatic system consists of the lymphatic vessels, tonsils, adenoids, spleen, and thymus gland. Lymphatic vessels are similar to the circulatory system's capillaries and veins and are connected to hundreds of lymph nodes within the body. Lymph nodes produce and store the cells that fight infection and disease. Tonsils take in bacteria and viruses that enter through the mouth and nose and are considered the first line of defense for the immune system. The spleen is the largest lymphatic organ and is responsible for producing both red and white blood cells and helps to detect dangerous microorganisms, viruses, and bacteria within the blood. As part of the immune system, the primary function of the lymphatic system is to transport a clear and colorless infection-fighting fluid called lymph, which contains white blood cells, throughout the body via the lymphatic vessels. Other functions of this system are absorbing fats and fat-soluble vitamins from the digestive system and transporting them into the bloodstream, restoring excess proteins and interstitial fluids to the blood, and helping to rid the body of toxic byproducts.

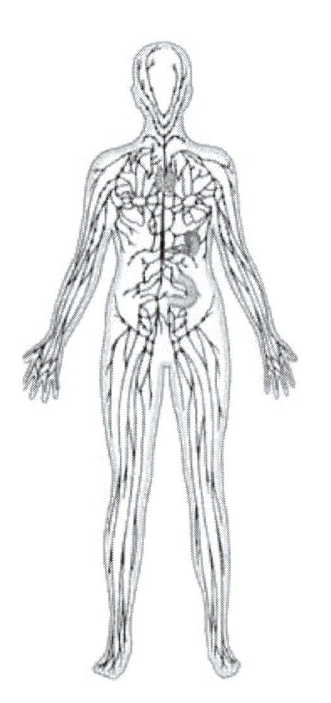

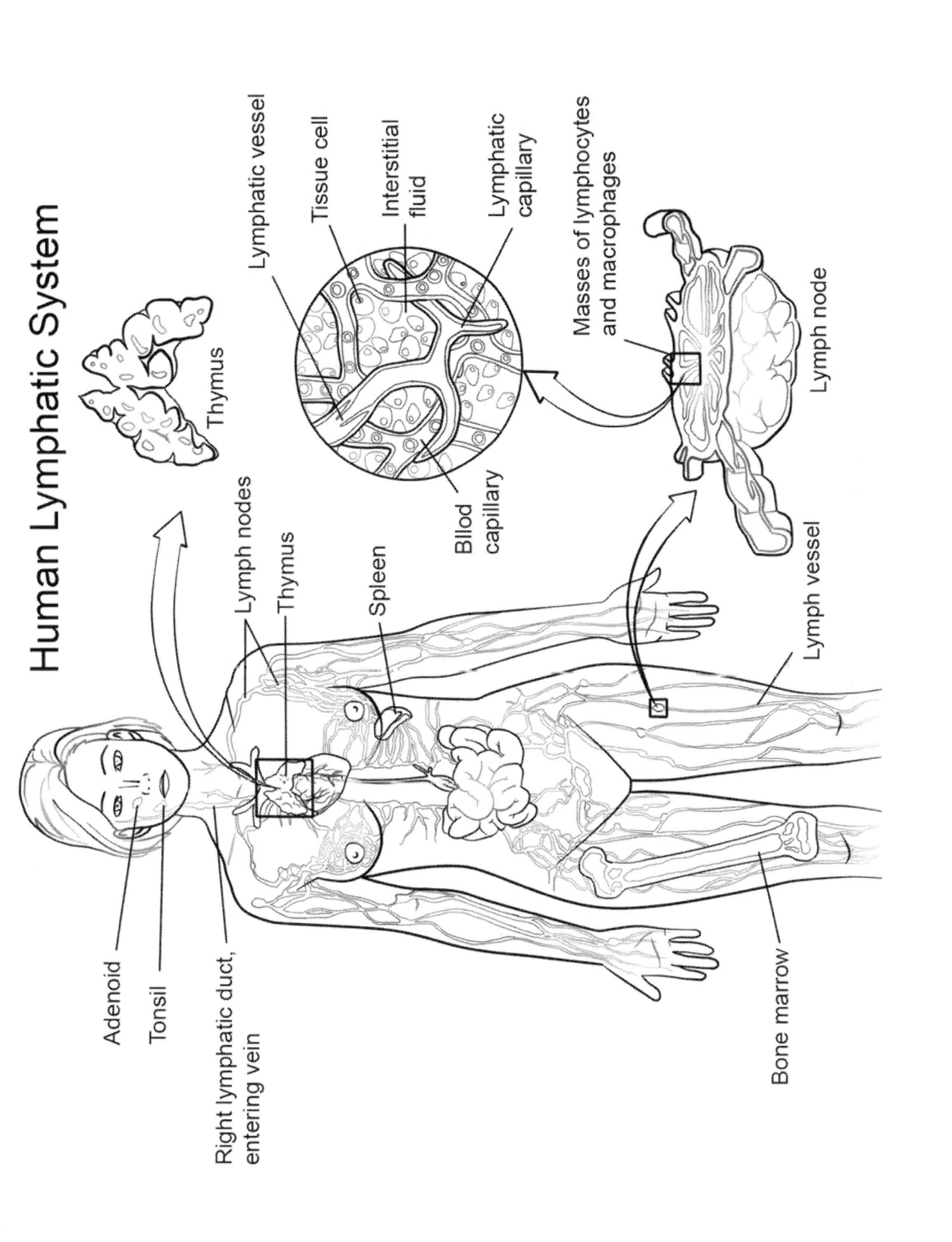

Human Lymphatic System

- Adenoid
- Tonsil
- Right lymphatic duct, entering vein
- Lymph nodes
- Thymus
- Spleen
- Bone marrow
- Thymus
- Lymphatic vessel
- Tissue cell
- Interstitial fluid
- Lymphatic capillary
- Blood capillary
- Masses of lymphocytes and macrophages
- Lymph node
- Lymph vessel

Reproductive systems

The reproductive system in men consists of the penis, scrotum, and testicles, and in women it consists of the ovaries, fallopian tubes, uterus, vagina, breasts, and mammary glands. Together there are four main functions of the reproductive system: the production of hormones such as testosterone, progesterone, and estrogen; the production of egg and sperm cells; the sustenance and transportation of these cells; and the development and nurturing of offspring. This system is vital to the survival of the human species by creating new life.

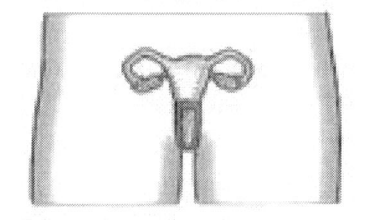

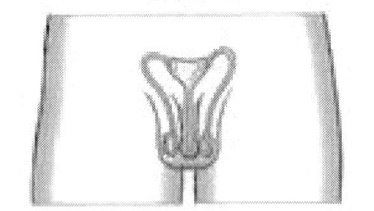

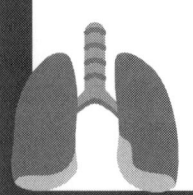

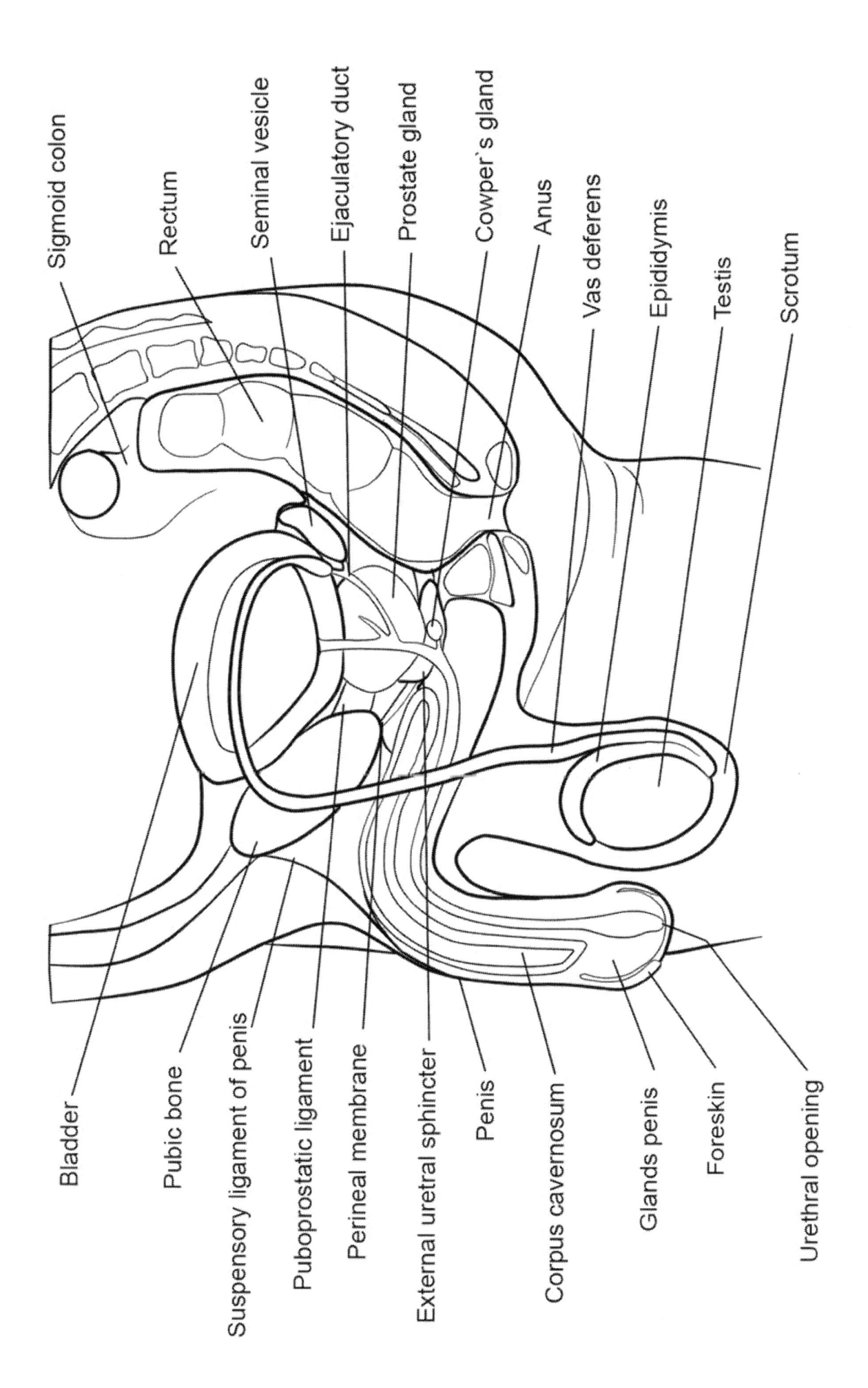

Male reproductive system

- Sigmoid colon
- Rectum
- Seminal vesicle
- Ejaculatory duct
- Prostate gland
- Cowper's gland
- Anus
- Vas deferens
- Epididymis
- Testis
- Scrotum
- Bladder
- Pubic bone
- Suspensory ligament of penis
- Puboprostatic ligament
- Perineal membrane
- External uretral sphincter
- Penis
- Corpus cavernosum
- Glands penis
- Foreskin
- Urethral opening

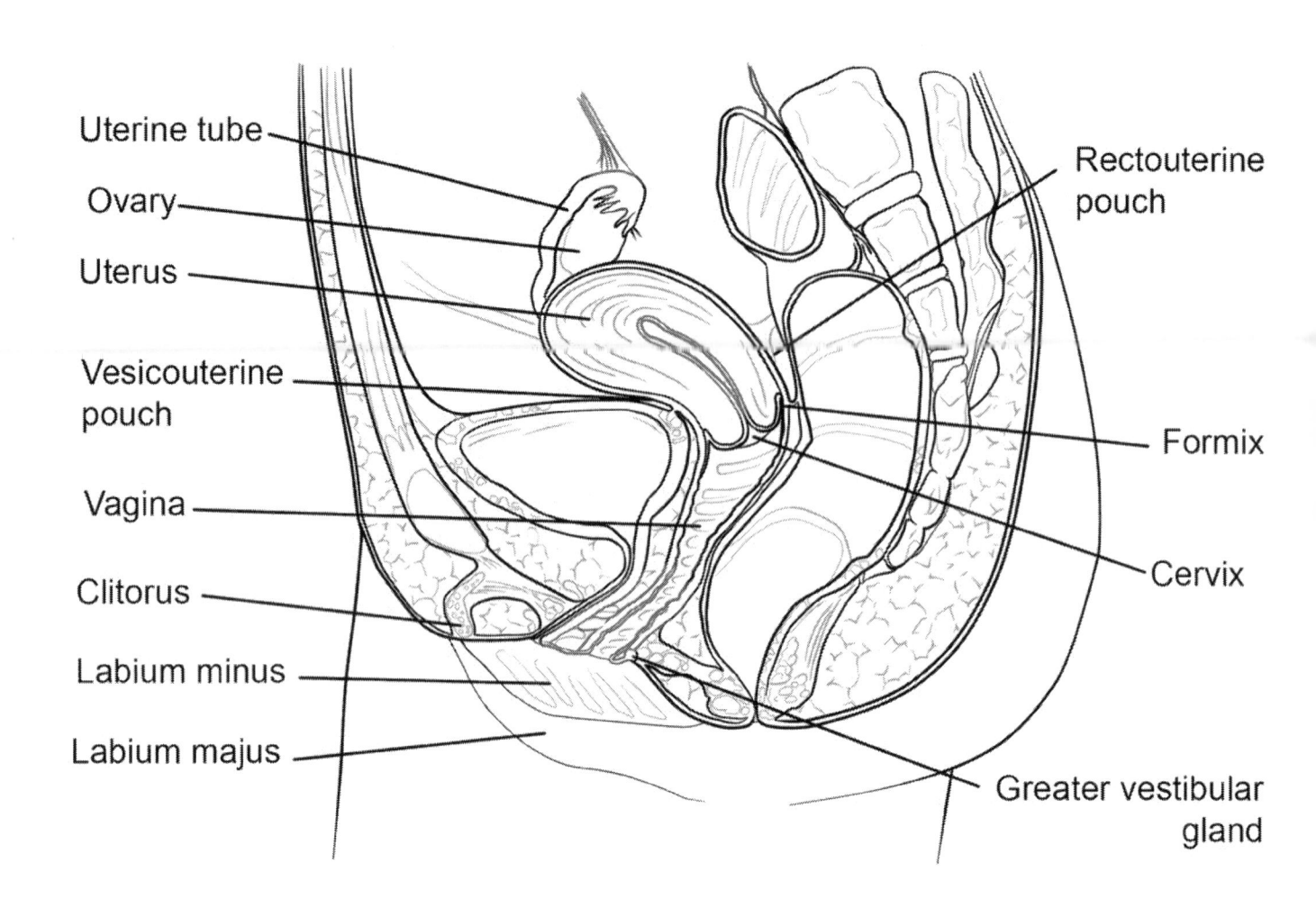

The Female Reproductive System

- Uterine tube
- Ovary
- Uterus
- Vesicouterine pouch
- Vagina
- Clitorus
- Labium minus
- Labium majus
- Rectouterine pouch
- Formix
- Cervix
- Greater vestibular gland

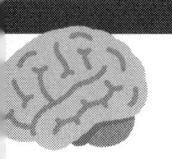

Urinary systems

The urinary system is made up of the kidneys, ureters, bladder, and urethra. The kidneys filter and remove extra fluid, toxins, and waste from the bloodstream in the form of urine. Every day this system produces at least 1 to 2 quarts of urine. Other primary functions of the urinary system are maintaining the body's relative state of homeostasis by keeping the levels of electrolytes in balance, producing hormones that regulate blood pressure, producing red blood cells, and helping to keep bones healthy by maintaining the right amounts of phosphorus and calcium within the body.

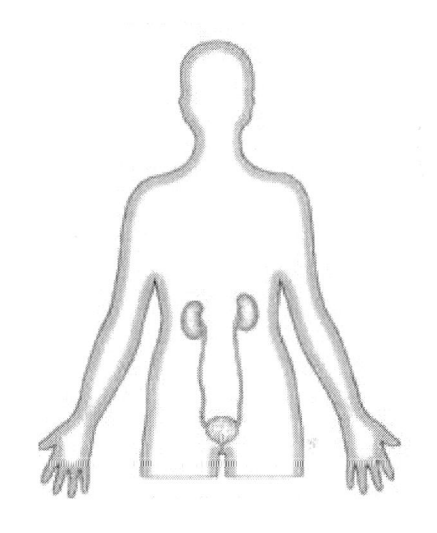

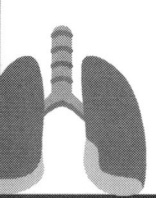

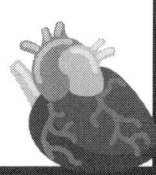

Kidney

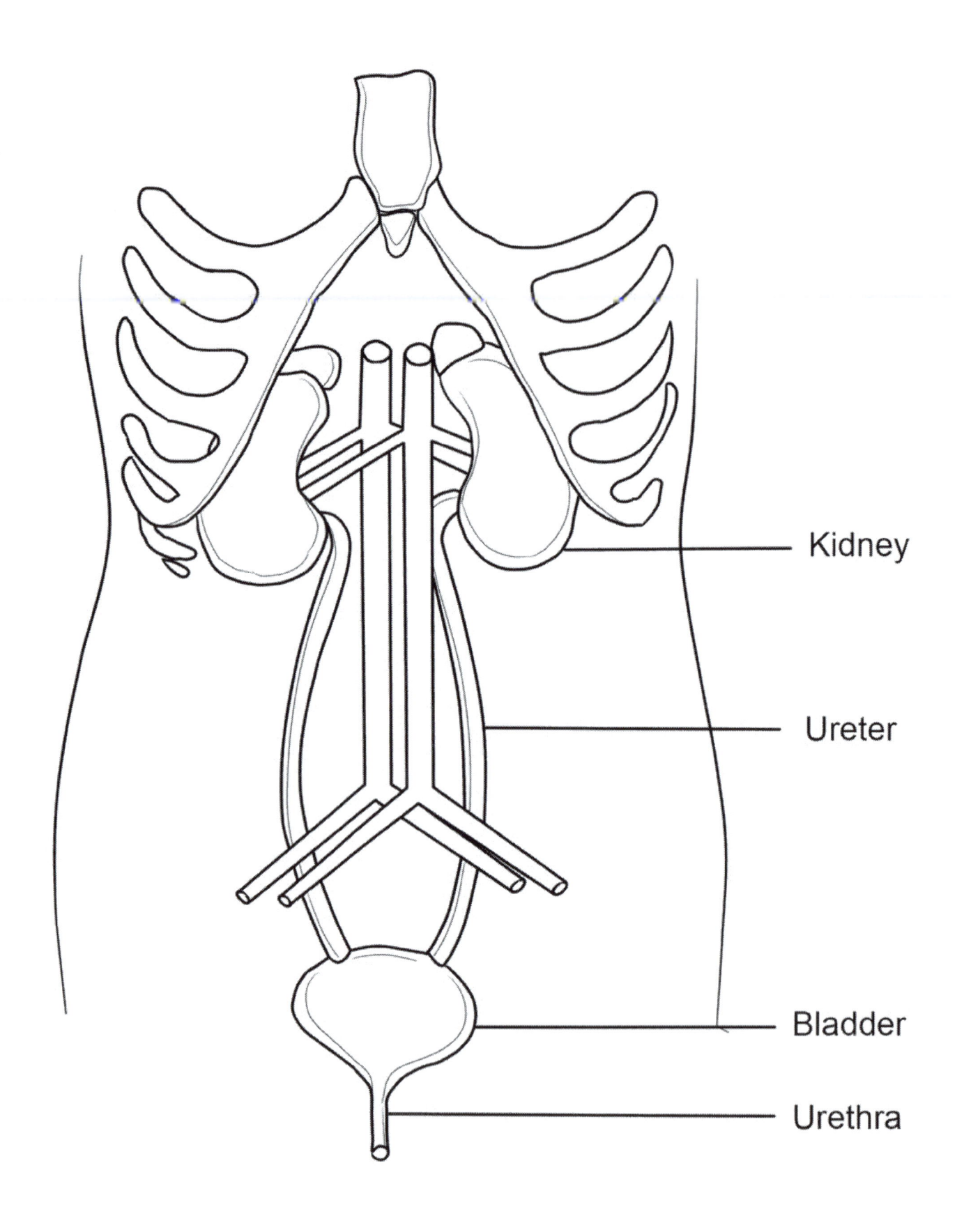

Ureter

Bladder

Urethra

The Urinary System

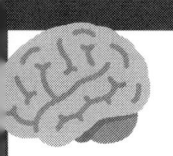

Mouth & tongue (oral cavity)

Anatomy of the oral cavity refers to mouth. The oral cavity includes the lips, hard palate (the bony front portion of the roof of the mouth), soft palate (the muscular back portion of the roof of the mouth), retromolar trigone (the area behind the wisdom teeth), front two-thirds of the tongue, gingiva (gums), buccal mucosa (the inner lining of the lips and cheeks), and floor of the mouth under the tongue.

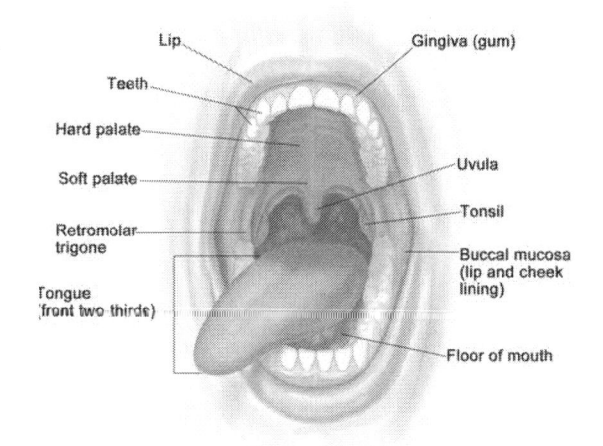

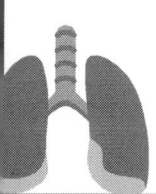

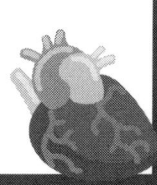

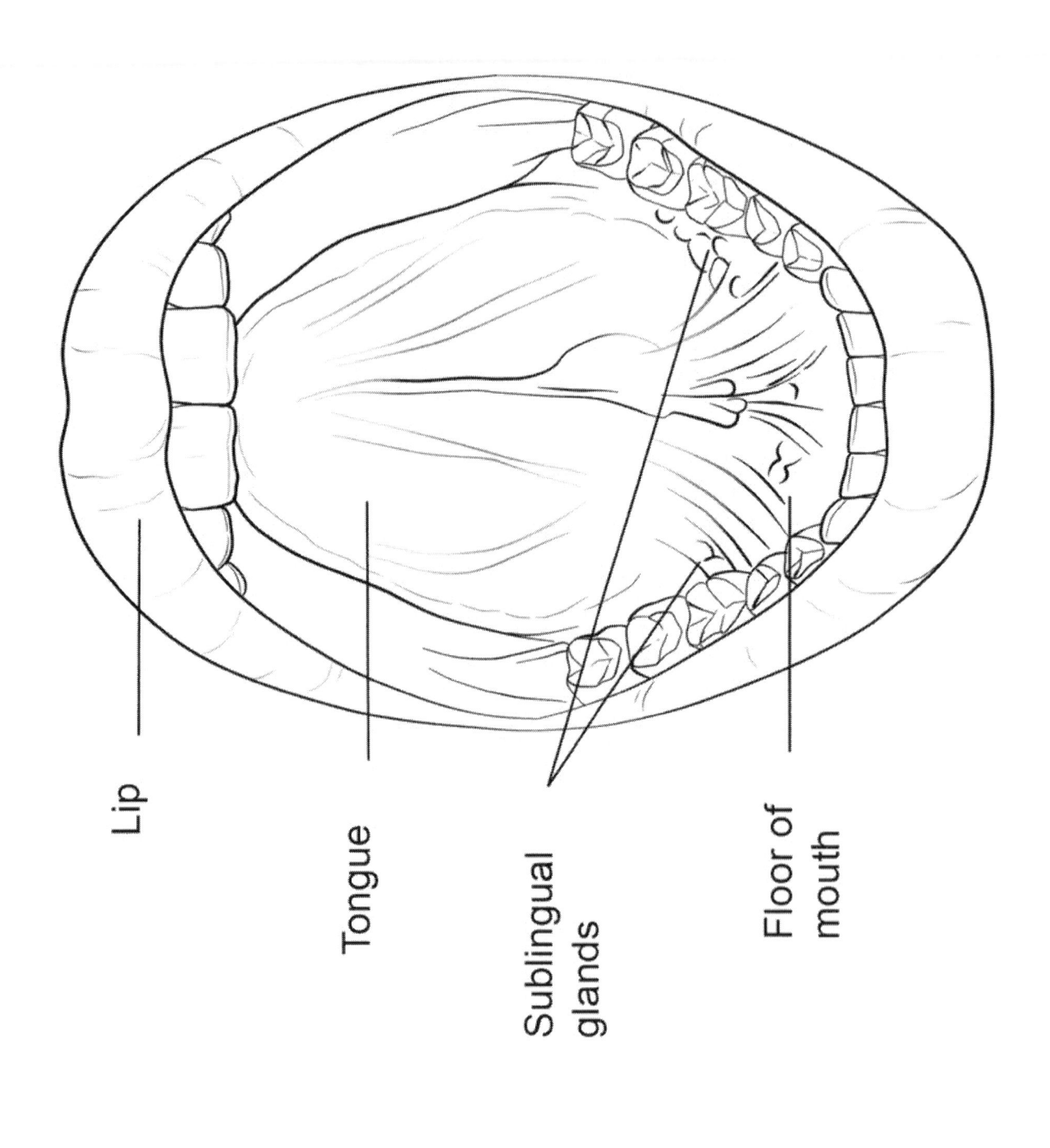

Human Mouth and Tongue

- Lip
- Tongue
- Sublingual glands
- Floor of mouth

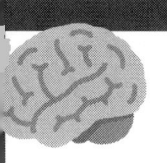

Anatomy of Eye

Iris: the colored partCornea: a clear dome over the irisPupil: the black circular opening in the iris that lets light inSclera: the white of your eyeConjunctiva: a thin layer of tissue that covers the entire front of your eye, except for the cornea.

Just behind the iris and pupil lies the lens, which helps focus light on the back of your eye. Most of the eye is filled with a clear gel called the vitreous. Light projects through your pupil and lens to the back of the eye. The inside lining of the eye is covered by special light-sensing cells that are collectively called the retina. It converts light into electrical impulses. Behind the eye, your optic nerve carries these impulses to the brain. The macula is a small extra-sensitive area in the retina that gives you central vision.

Eye color is created by the amount and type of pigment in your iris. Multiple genes inherited from each parent determine a person's eye color.

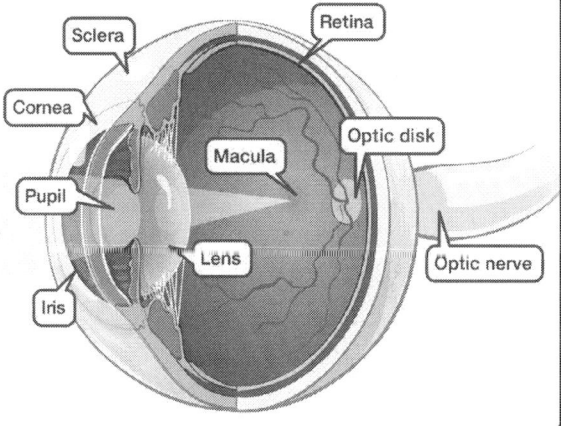

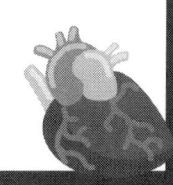

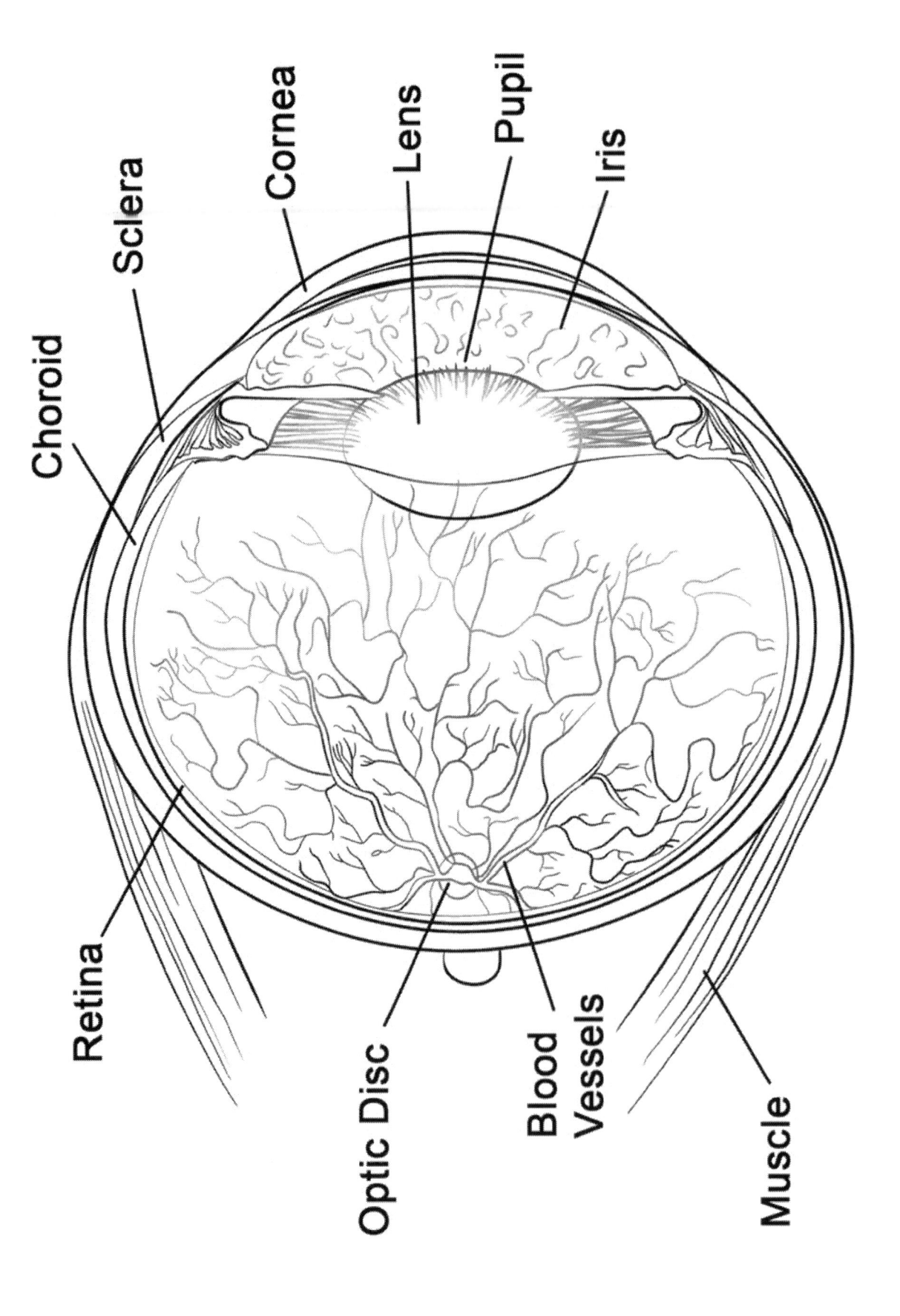

Cornea
Sclera
Lens
Pupil
Iris
Choroid
Retina
Optic Disc
Blood Vessels
Muscle

Anatomy of the Eye

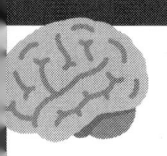

Anatomy of Skin

The skin is the body's largest organ. It covers the entire body. It serves as a protective shield against heat, light, injury, and infection. The skin also:Regulates body temperatureStores water and fatIs a sensory organPrevents water lossPrevents entry of bacteriaActs as a barrier between the organism and its environmentHelps to make vitamin D when exposed to the sunYour skin takes on different thickness, color, and texture all over your body. For example, your head contains more hair follicles than anywhere else. But the soles of your feet have none. In addition, the soles of your feet and the palms of your hands are much thicker than skin on other areas of your body.The skin is made up of 3 layers. Each layer has certain functions:EpidermisDermisSubcutaneous fat layer (hypodermis).

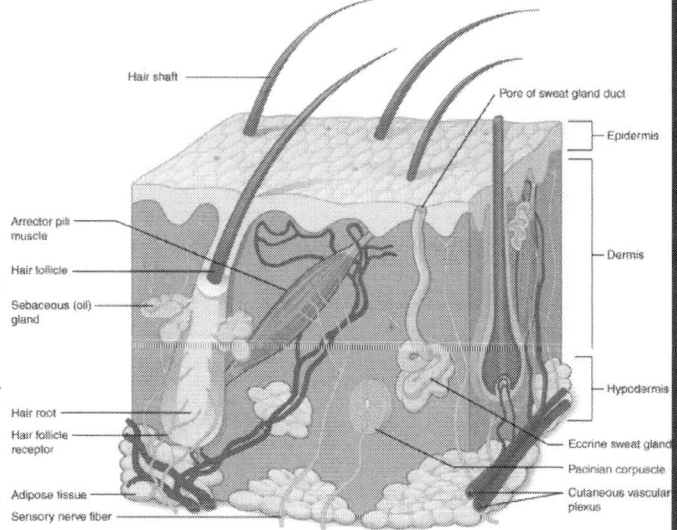

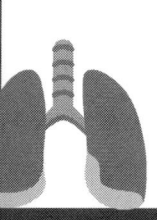

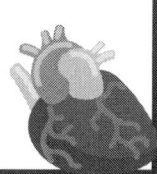

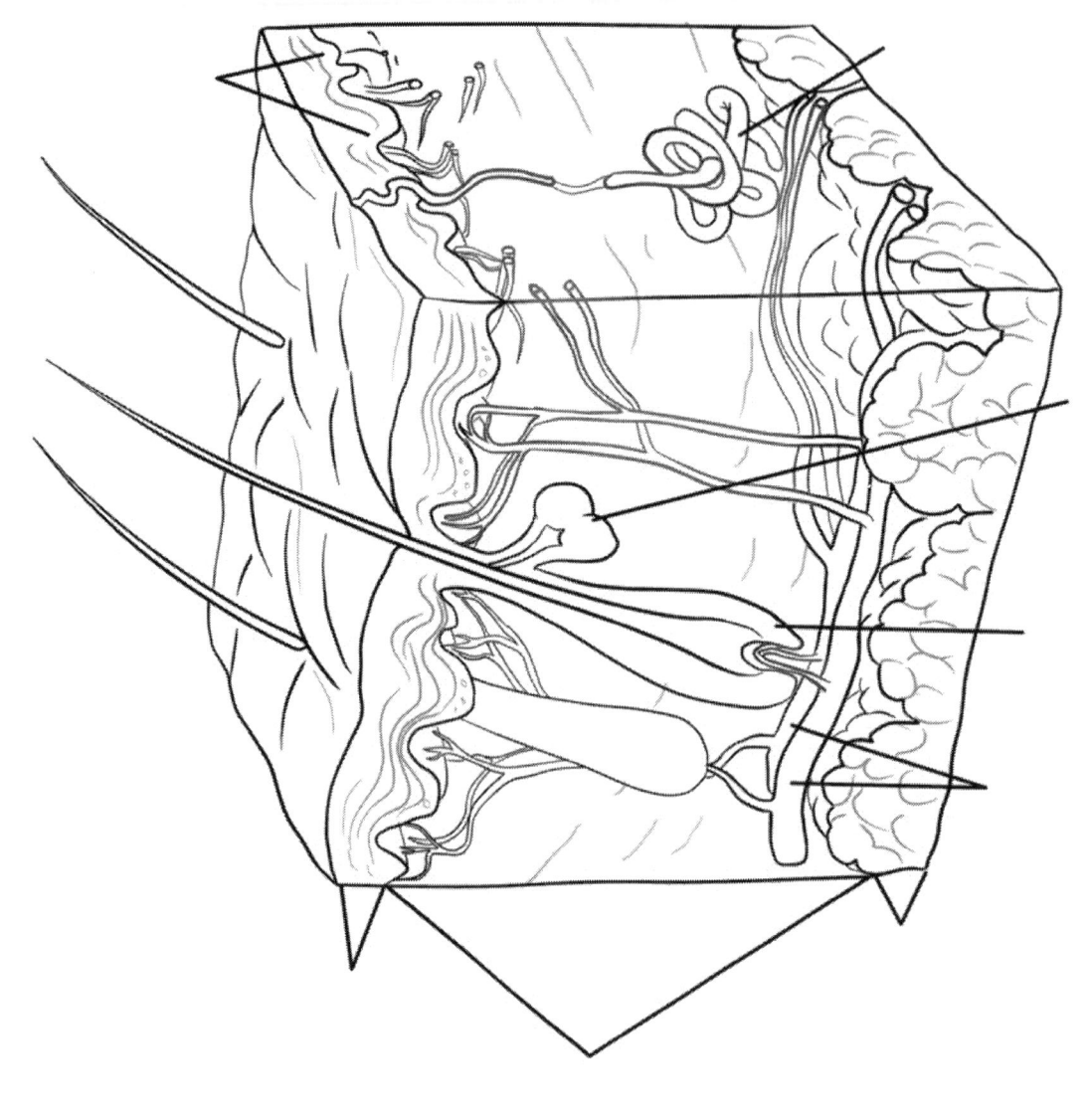

Word Bank
1. Epidermis
2. Blood vessels
3. Fatty Tissue
4. Oil
5. Follicle
6. Dermis
7. Melanocytes
8. Sweat gland

The Human Skin

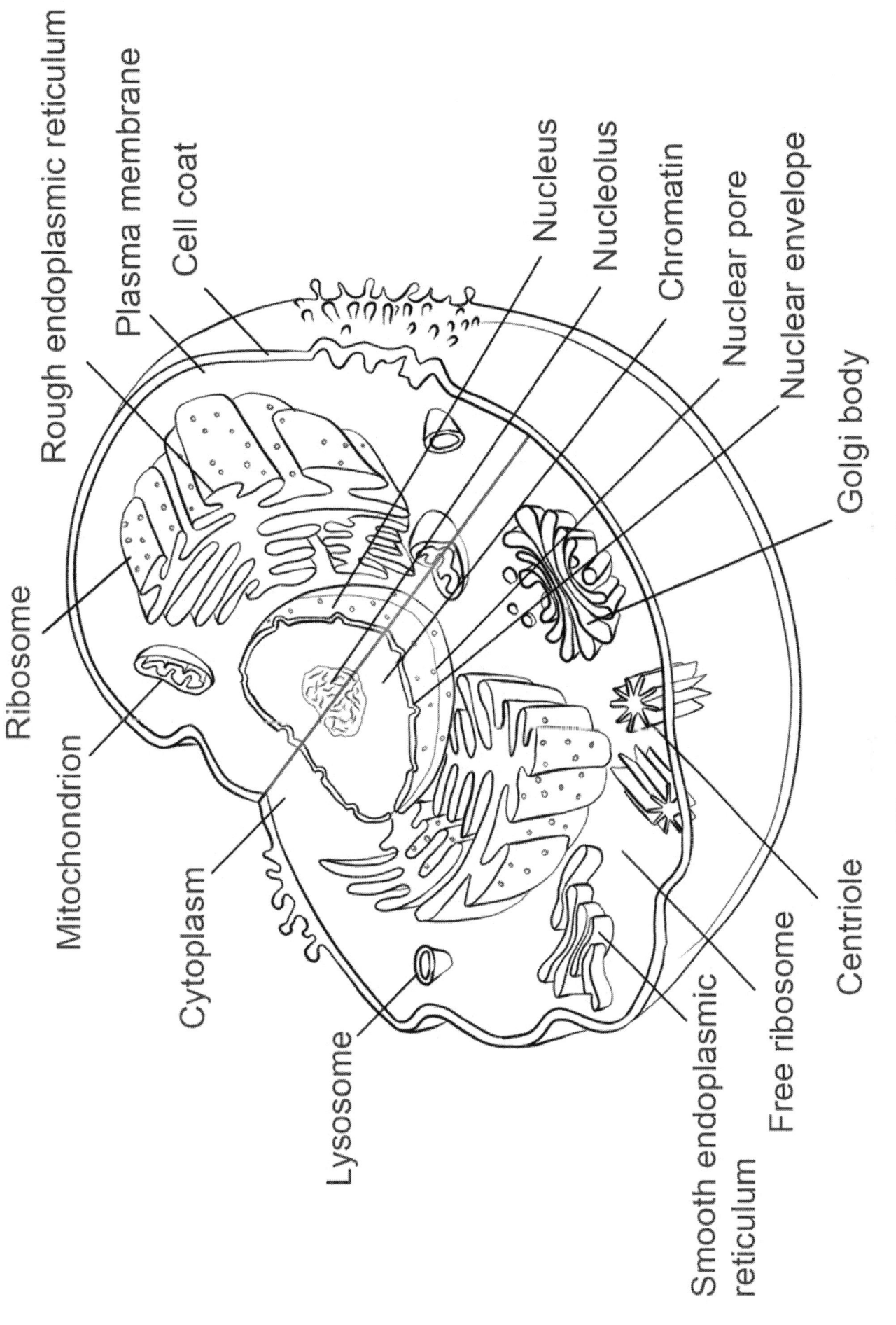

The Human Cell

- Ribosome
- Rough endoplasmic reticulum
- Plasma membrane
- Cell coat
- Nucleus
- Nucleolus
- Chromatin
- Nuclear pore
- Nuclear envelope
- Golgi body
- Mitochondrion
- Cytoplasm
- Lysosome
- Smooth endoplasmic reticulum
- Free ribosome
- Centriole

Immune system

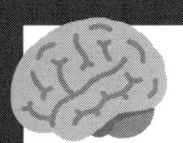

Immune system, the complex group of defense responses found in humans and other advanced vertebrates that helps repel disease-causing organisms (pathogens). Immunity from disease is actually conferred by two cooperative defense systems, called nonspecific, innate immunity and specific, acquired immunity. Nonspecific protective mechanisms repel all microorganisms equally, while the specific immune responses are tailored to particular types of invaders. Both systems work together to thwart organisms from entering and proliferating within the body. These immune mechanisms also help eliminate abnormal cells of the body that can develop into cancer.

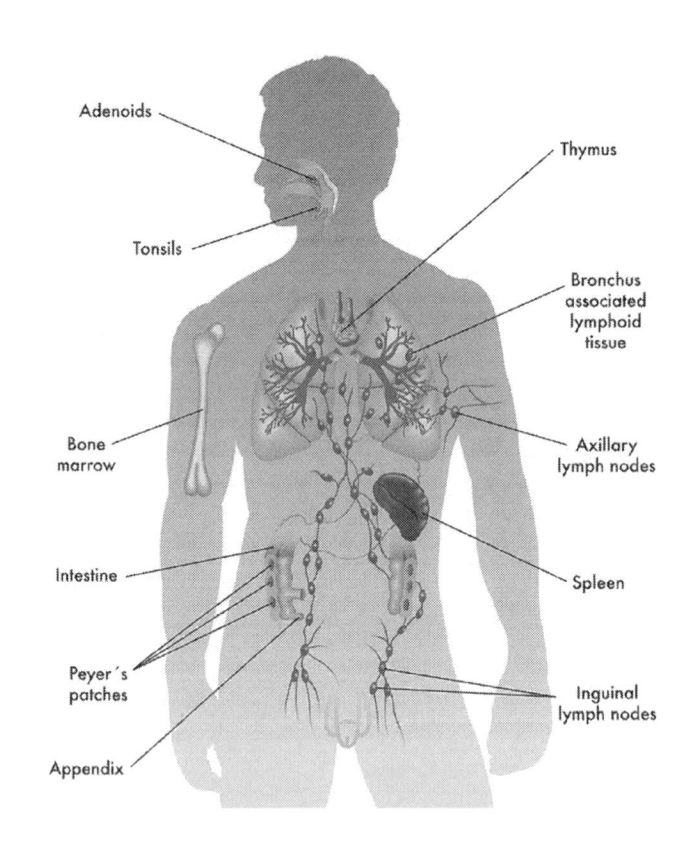

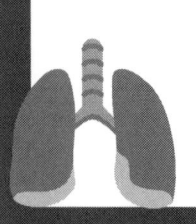

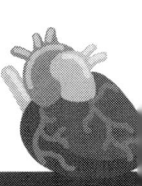

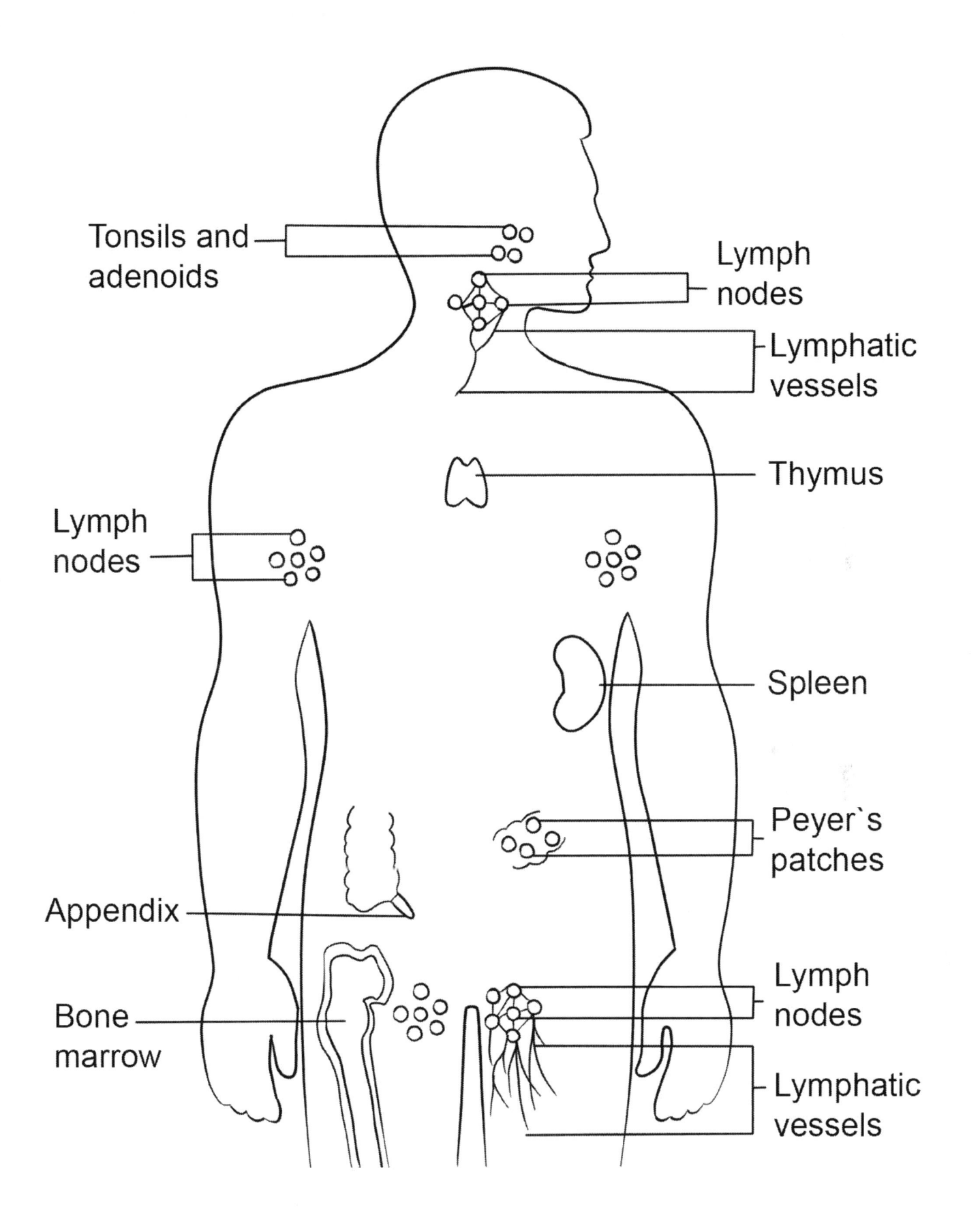

Human Immune System

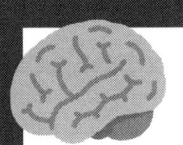

Central nervous system

The central nervous system consists of the brain and spinal cord. It is referred to as "central" because it combines information from the entire body and coordinates activity across the whole organs. CNS consists of the brain and spinal cord.

CNS consists of the brain and spinal cord. The brain is the most complex organ in the body and uses 20 percent of the total oxygen we breathe in. The brain consists of an estimated 100 billion neurons, with each connected to thousands more. The brain can be divided into four main lobes: temporal, parietal, occipital and frontal.

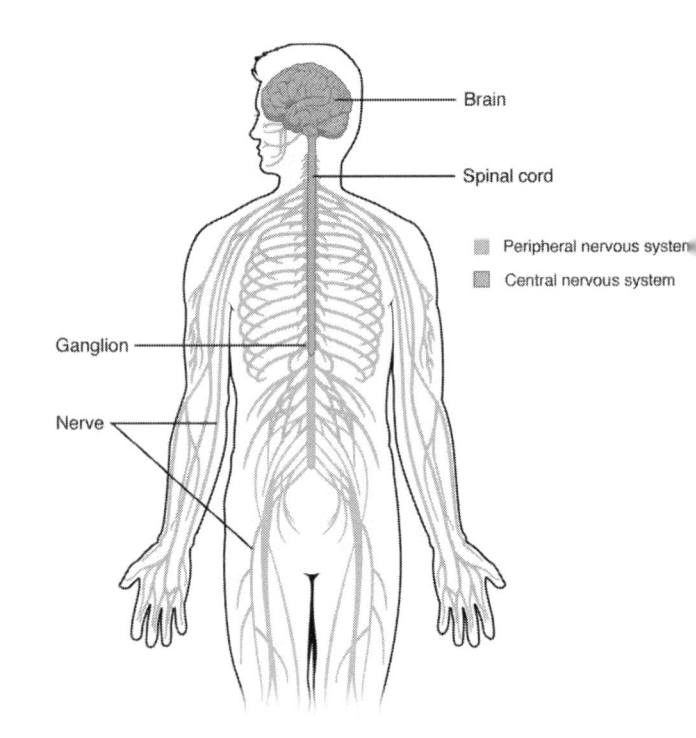

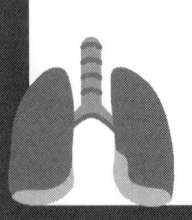

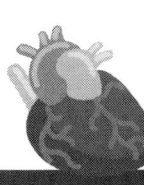

Central Nervous System

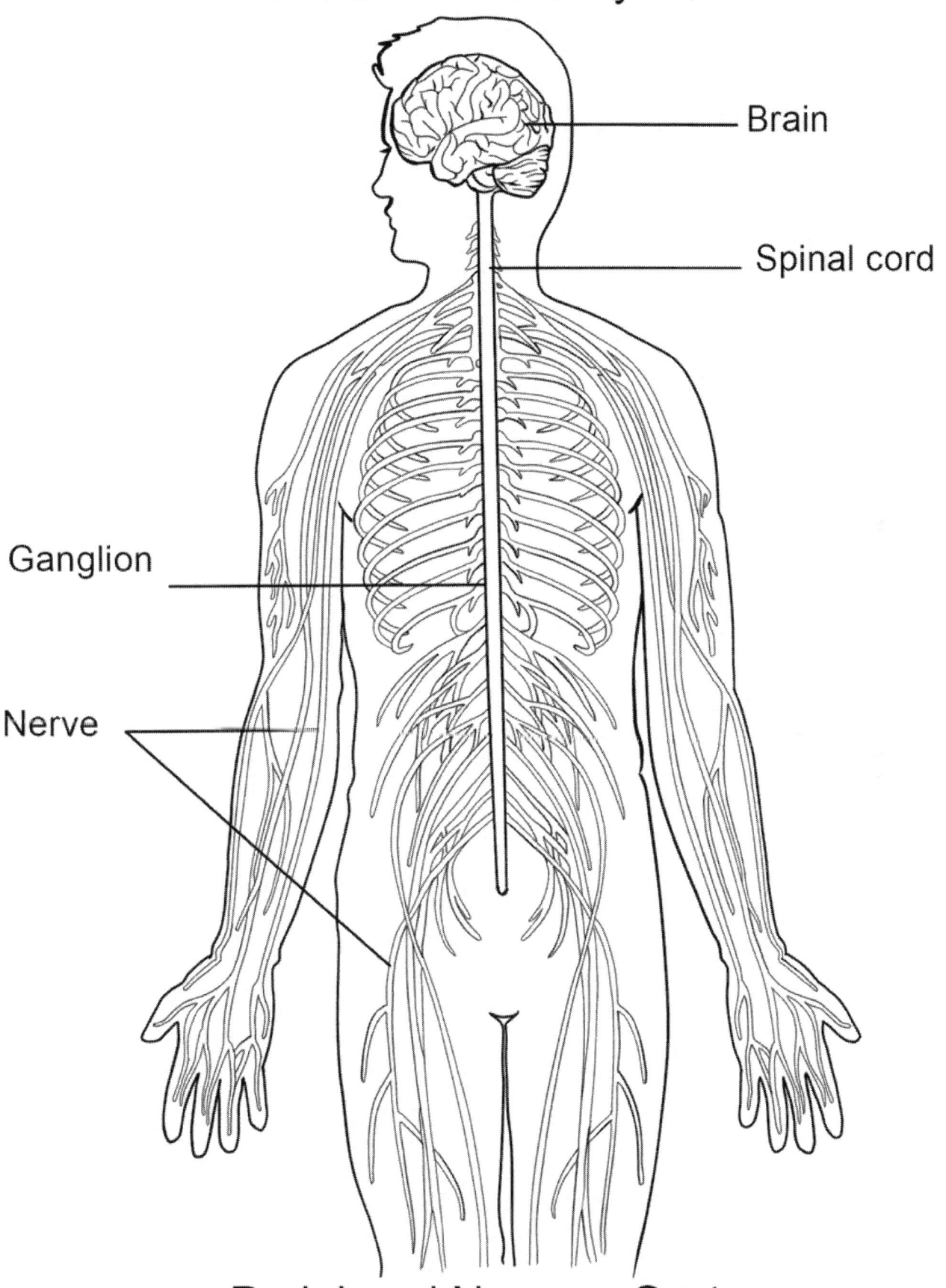

- Brain
- Spinal cord
- Ganglion
- Nerve

Peripheral Nervous System

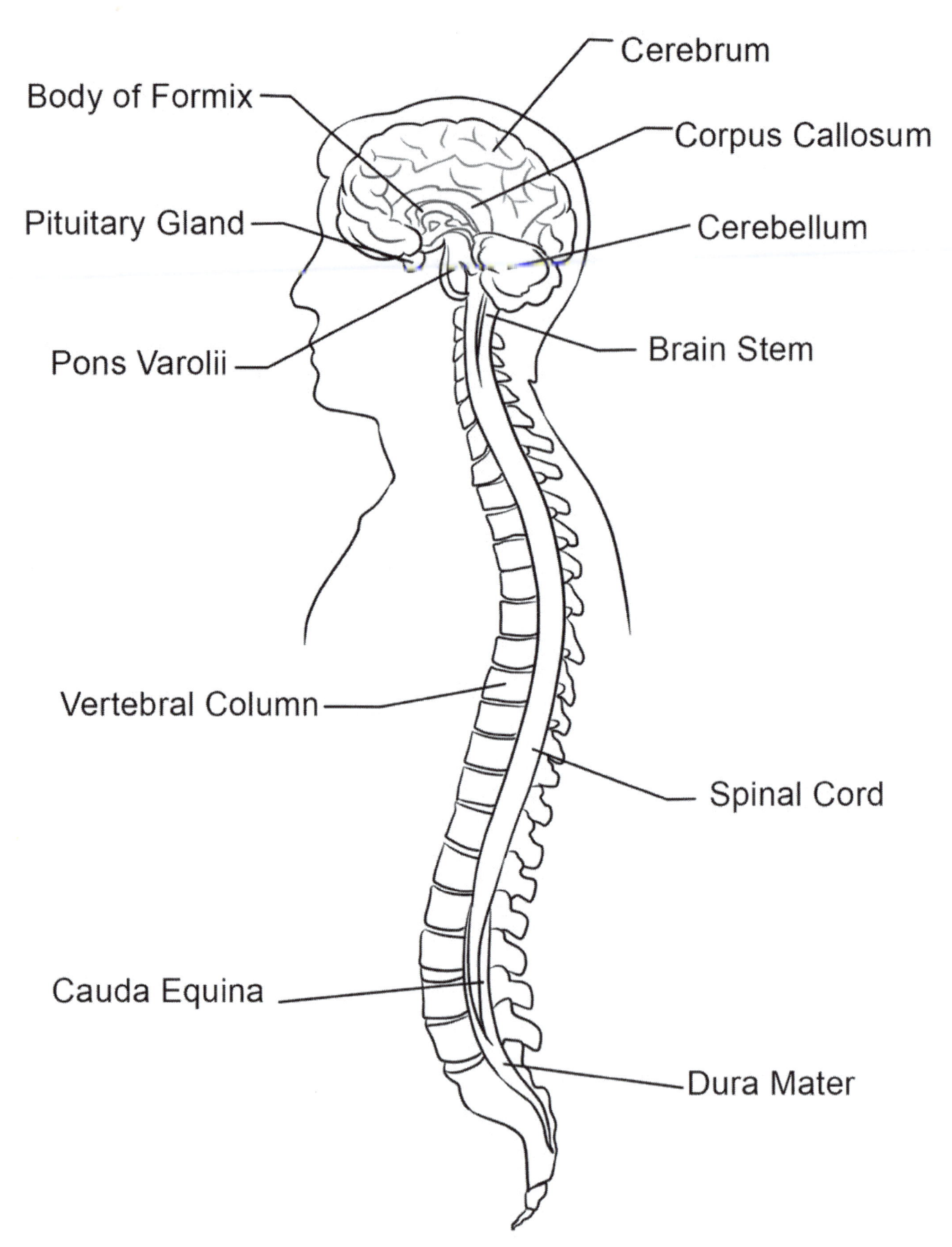

- Body of Formix
- Pituitary Gland
- Pons Varolii
- Vertebral Column
- Cauda Equina
- Cerebrum
- Corpus Callosum
- Cerebellum
- Brain Stem
- Spinal Cord
- Dura Mater

Central Nervous System

Human Brain

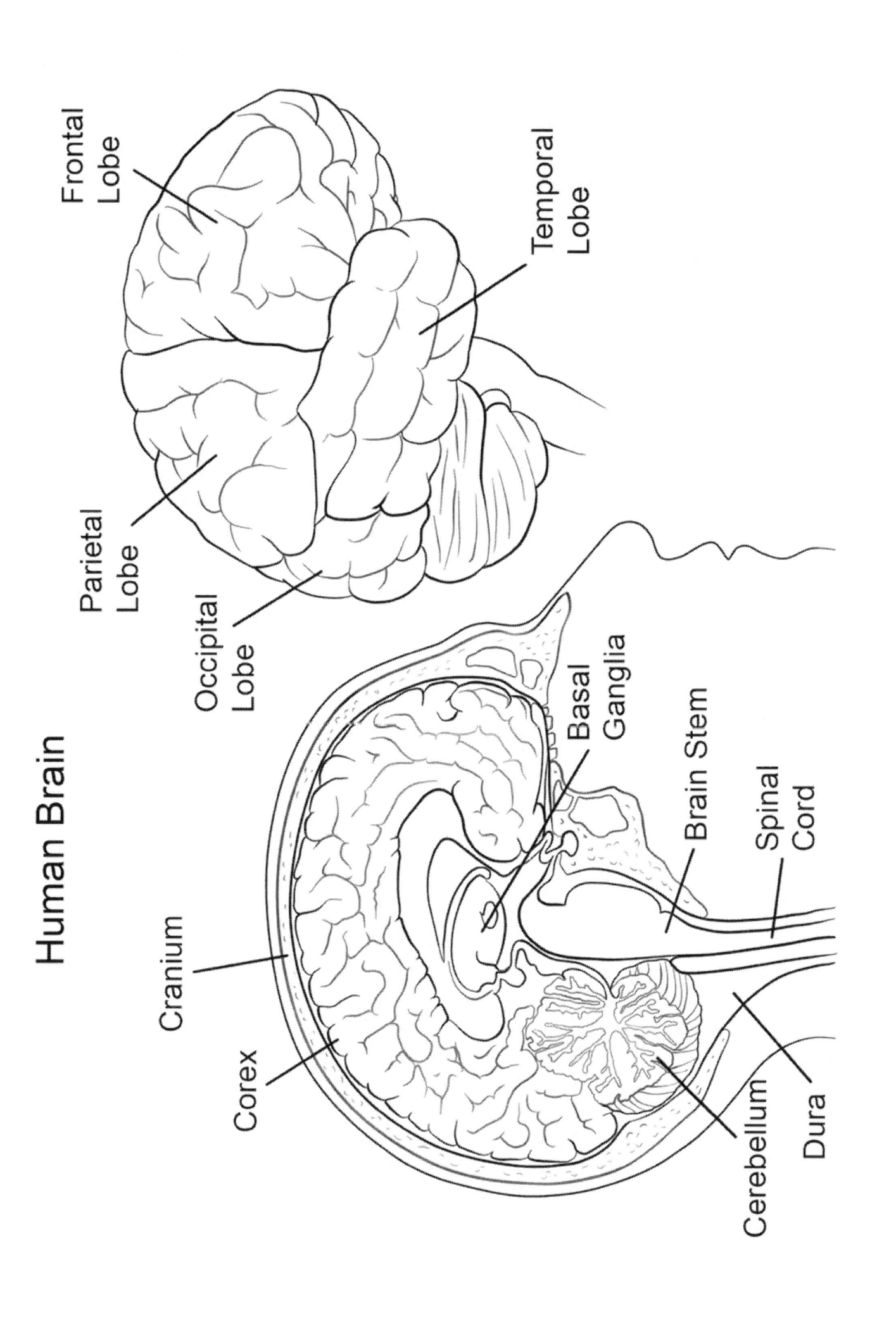

- Frontal Lobe
- Temporal Lobe
- Parietal Lobe
- Occipital Lobe
- Cranium
- Corex
- Basal Ganglia
- Brain Stem
- Spinal Cord
- Cerebellum
- Dura

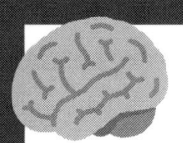

Anatomy of Leg

the upper limb, the lower limb is divided into three regions. The thigh is that portion of the lower limb located between the hip joint and knee joint. The leg is specifically the region between the knee joint and the ankle joint. Distal to the ankle is the foot. The lower limb contains 30 bones. These are the femur, patella, tibia, fibula, tarsal bones, metatarsal bones, and phalanges

The femur is the single bone of the thigh. The patella is the kneecap and articulates with the distal femur. The tibia is the larger, weight-bearing bone located on the medial side of the leg, and the fibula is the thin bone of the lateral leg. The bones of the foot are divided into three groups. The posterior portion of the foot is formed by a group of seven bones, each of which is known as a tarsal bone, whereas the mid-foot contains five elongated bones, each of which is a metatarsal bone. The toes contain 14 small bones, each of which is a phalanx bone of the foot.

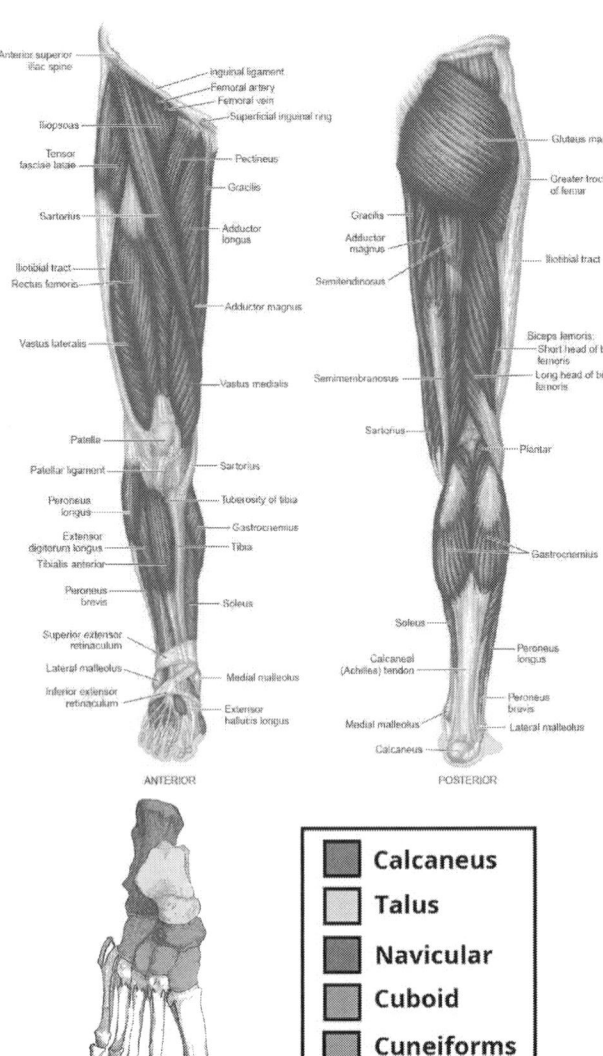

Biceps femoris

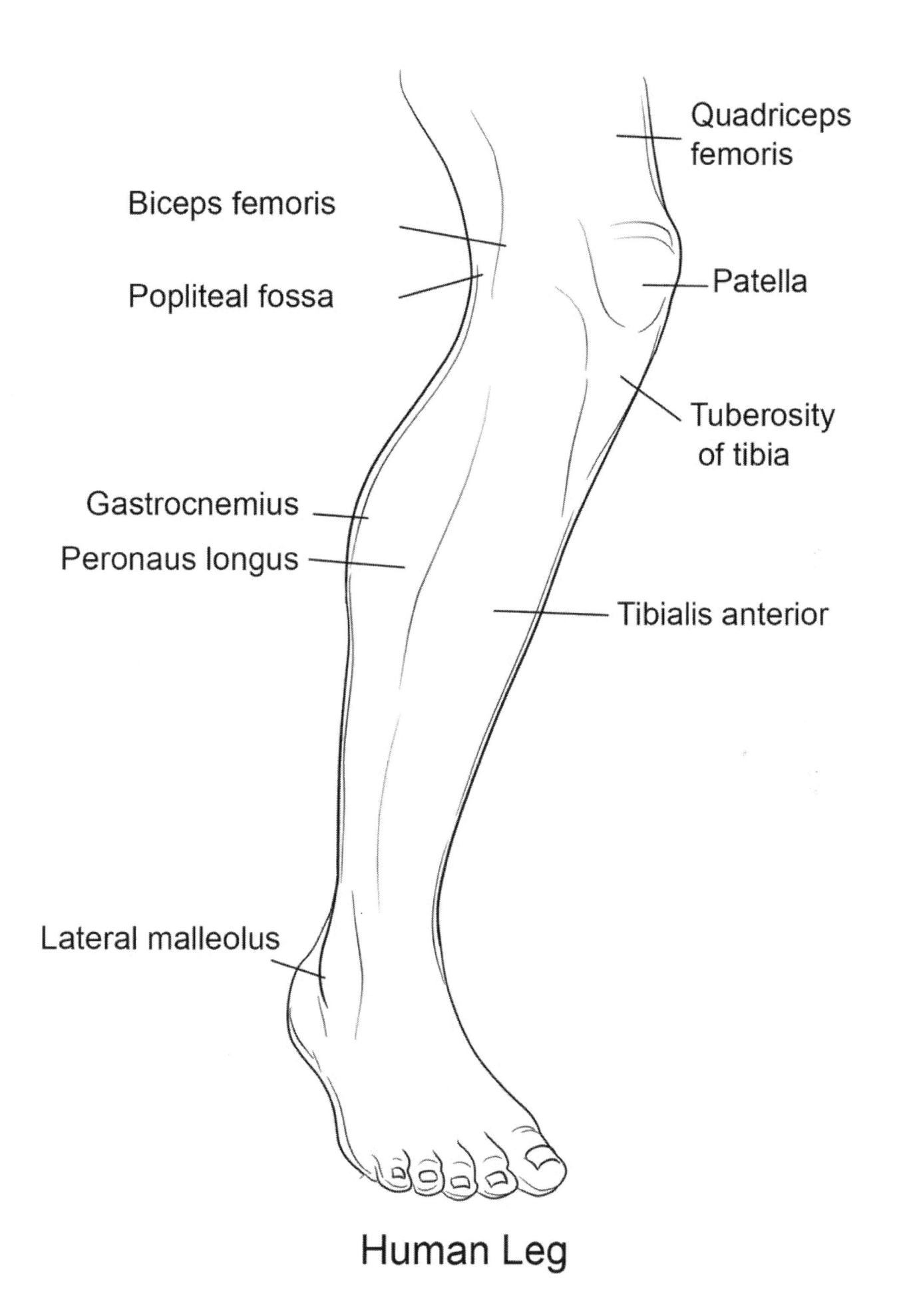

Popliteal fossa

Gastrocnemius

Peronaus longus

Lateral malleolus

Quadriceps femoris

Patella

Tuberosity of tibia

Tibialis anterior

Human Leg

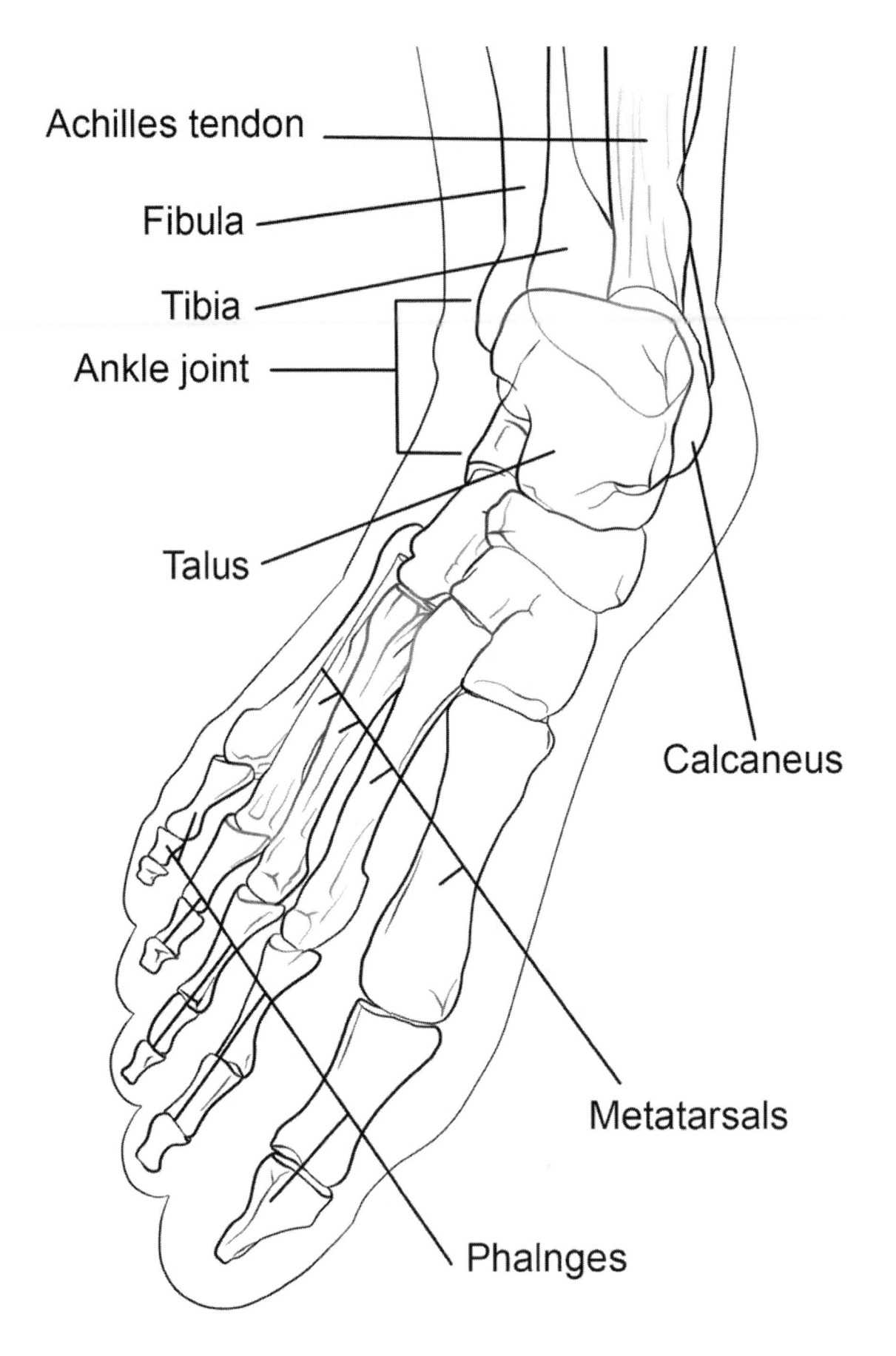

Achilles tendon
Fibula
Tibia
Ankle joint
Talus
Calcaneus
Metatarsals
Phalnges

Lower Leg and Foot

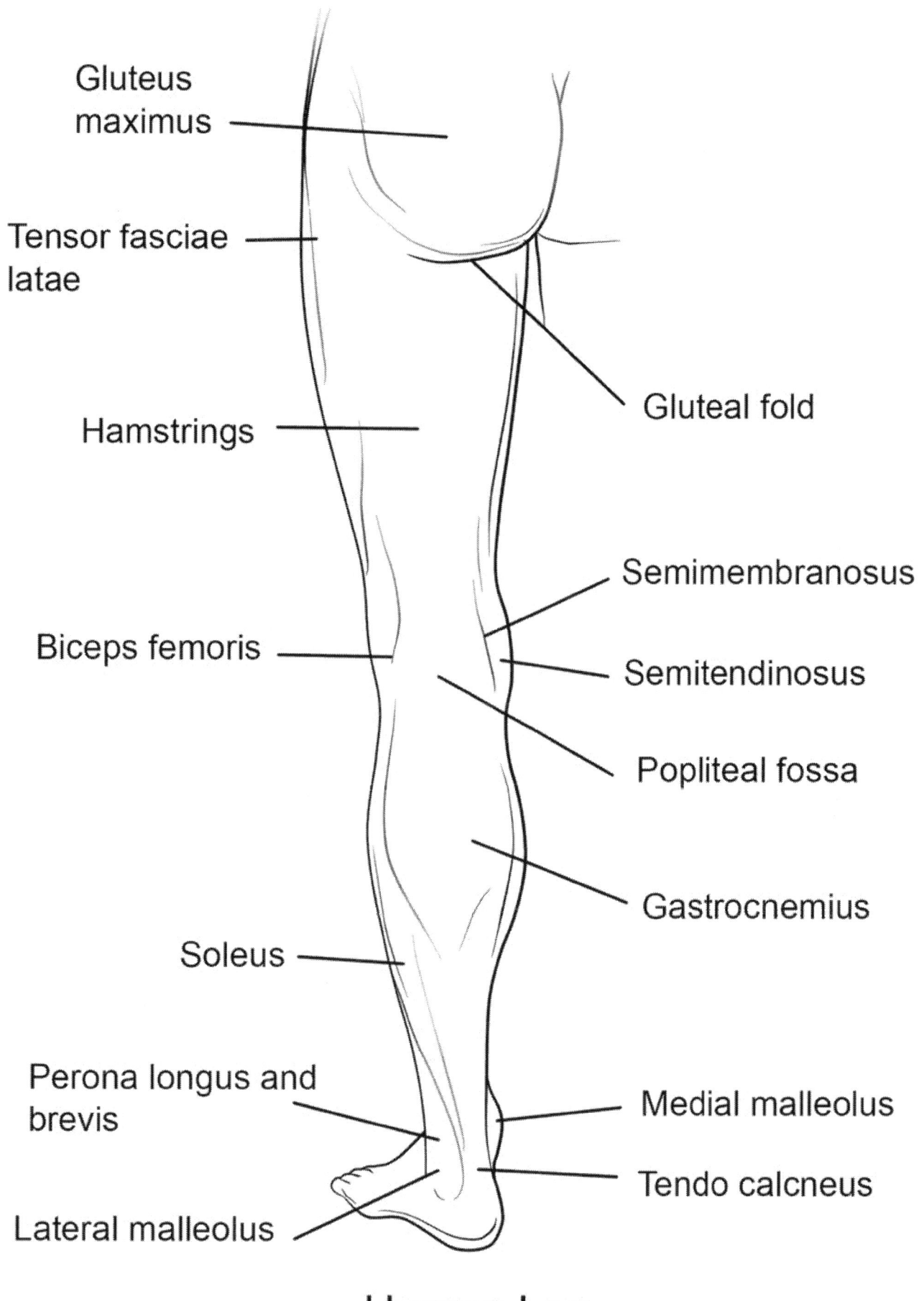

Gluteus maximus	
Tensor fasciae latae	
	Gluteal fold
Hamstrings	
	Semimembranosus
Biceps femoris	Semitendinosus
	Popliteal fossa
	Gastrocnemius
Soleus	
Perona longus and brevis	Medial malleolus
	Tendo calcneus
Lateral malleolus	

Human Leg

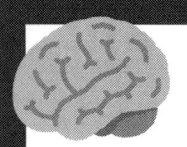

Anatomy of Hand

The hand is made up of many bones: 5 elongated metacarpal bones, which are next to the wrist and help to make up the palm; 14 phalanges which make up the fingers. Each finger is made up of 3 phalanges; the thumb is made up of 2. These 19 bones collectively form 14 separate joints. The knuckles, known as the metacarpophalangeal (MCP) joints, join the fingers to the palm. The interphalangeal (IP) joints are the finger joints. All of these small joints are known as synovial joints and are covered with articular cartilage.

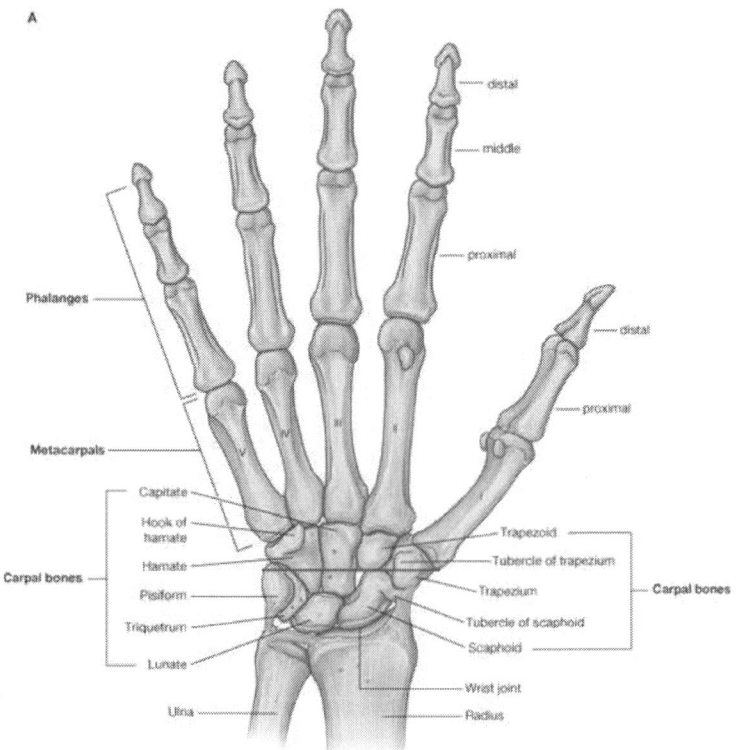

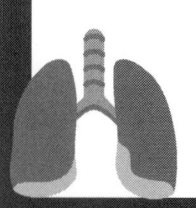

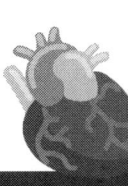

Bones of the hand and wrist

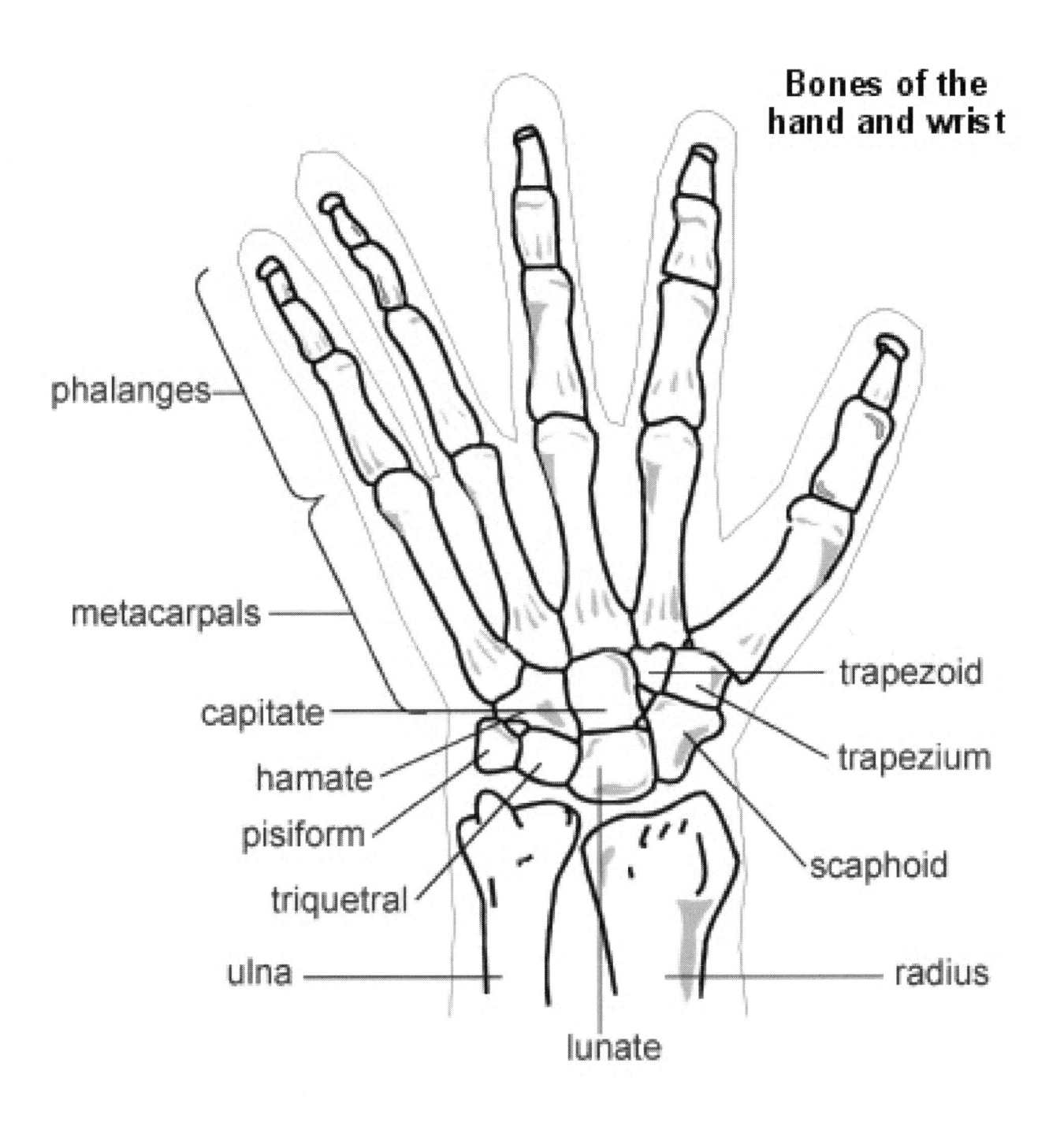

WORKSHEETS

BODY ORGANS
Color the body organs

1. HEART

2. LUNGS

3. LIVER

4. STOMACH

5. LARGE INTESTINE

6. SMALL INTESTINE

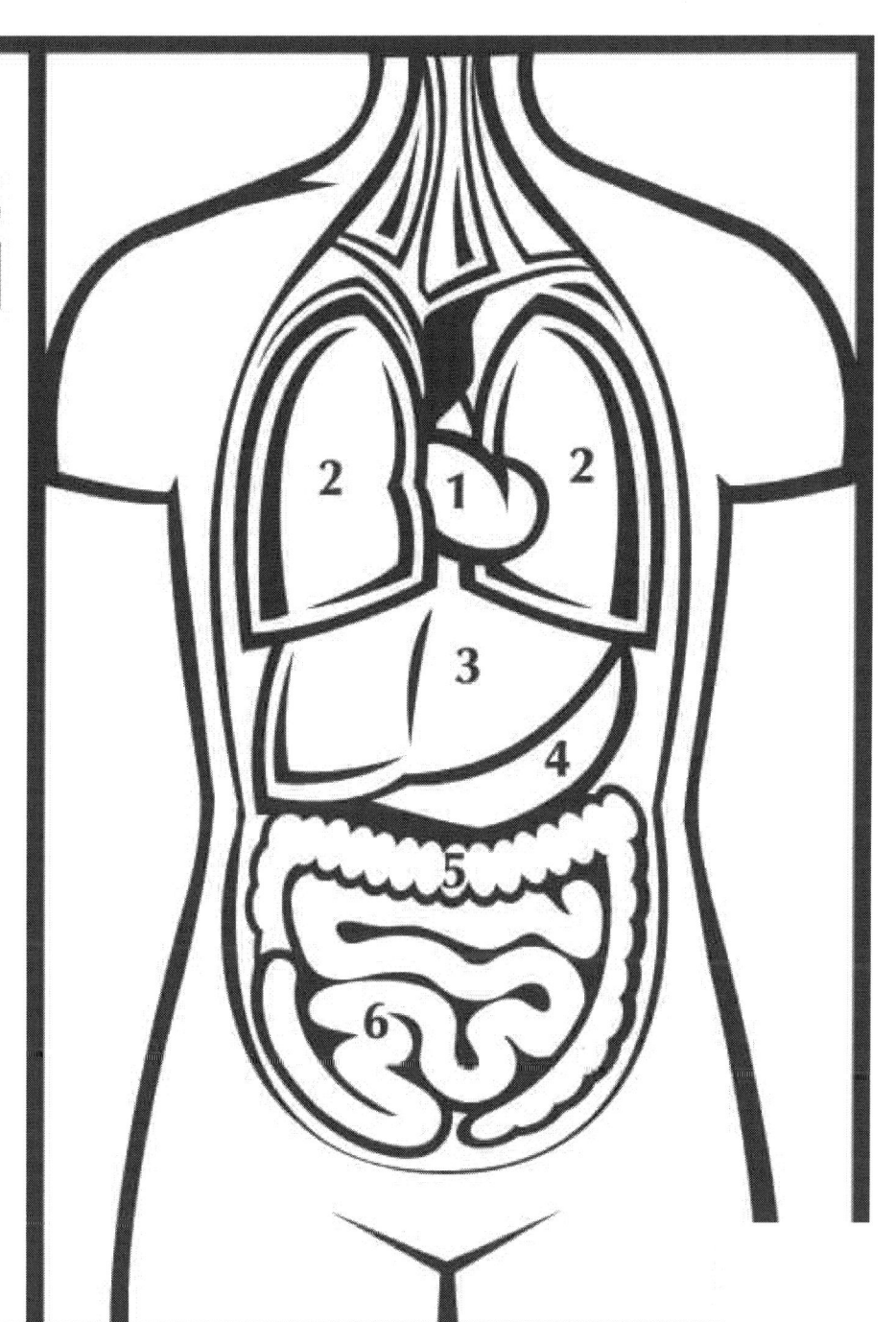

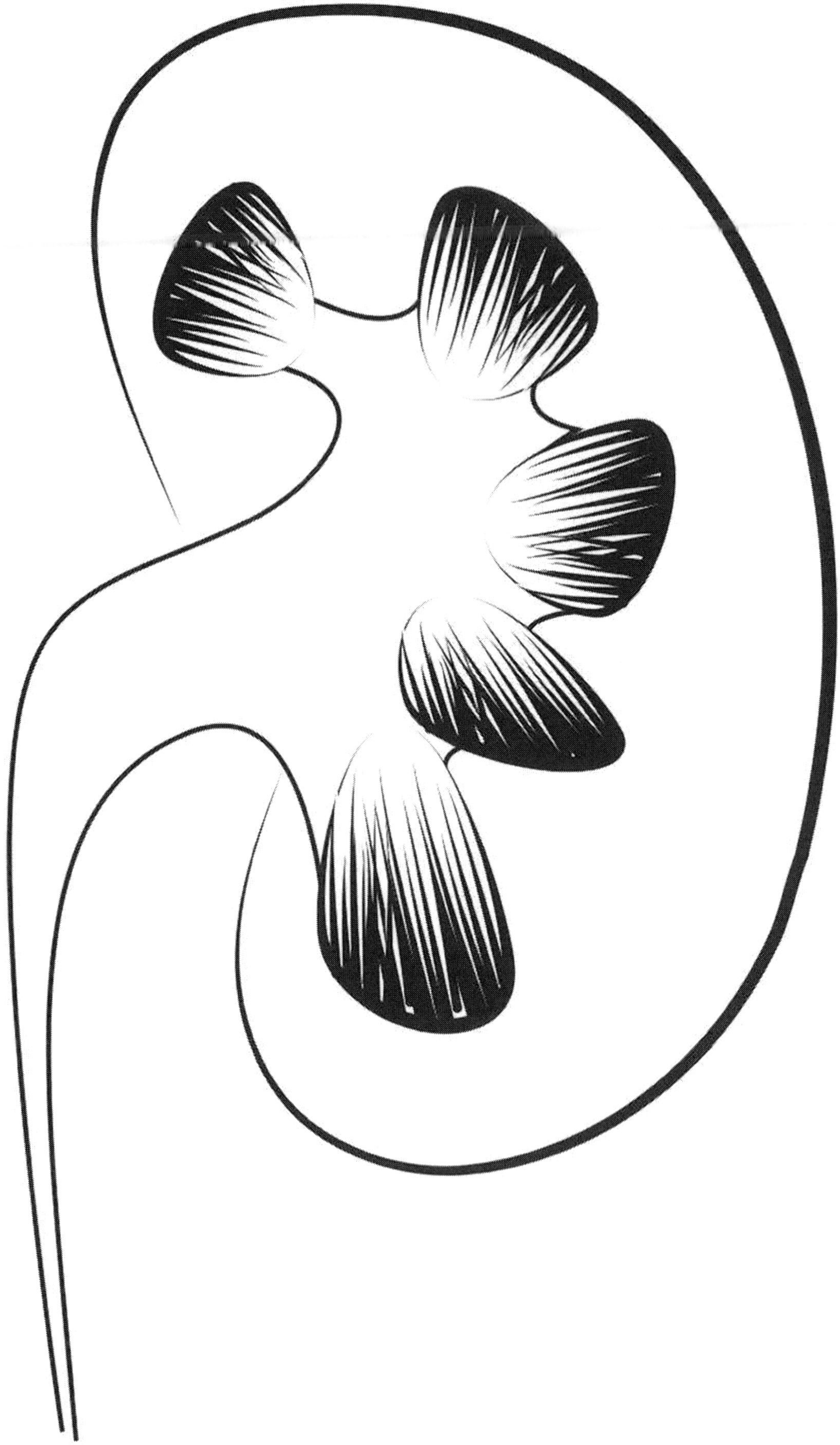

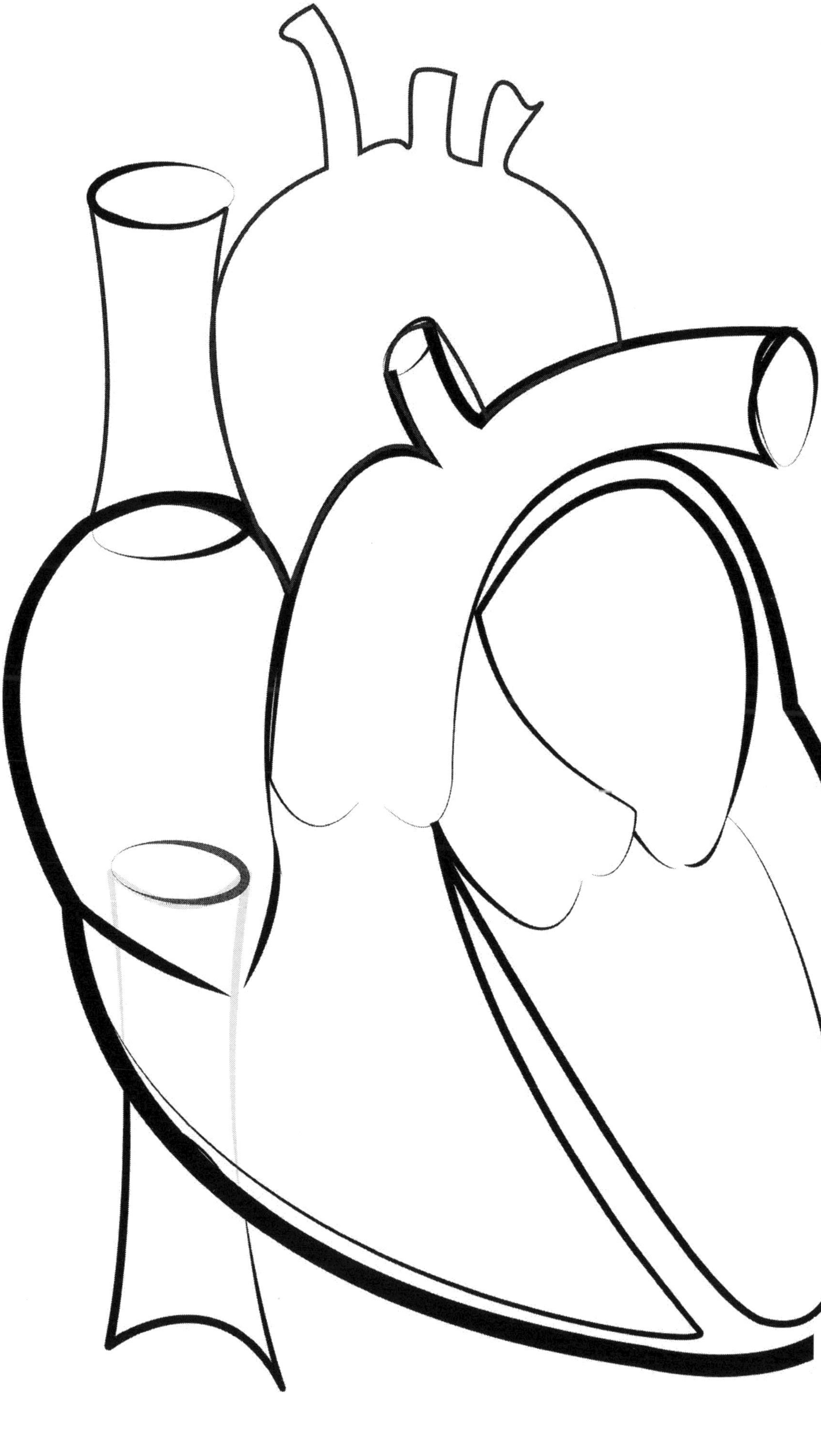

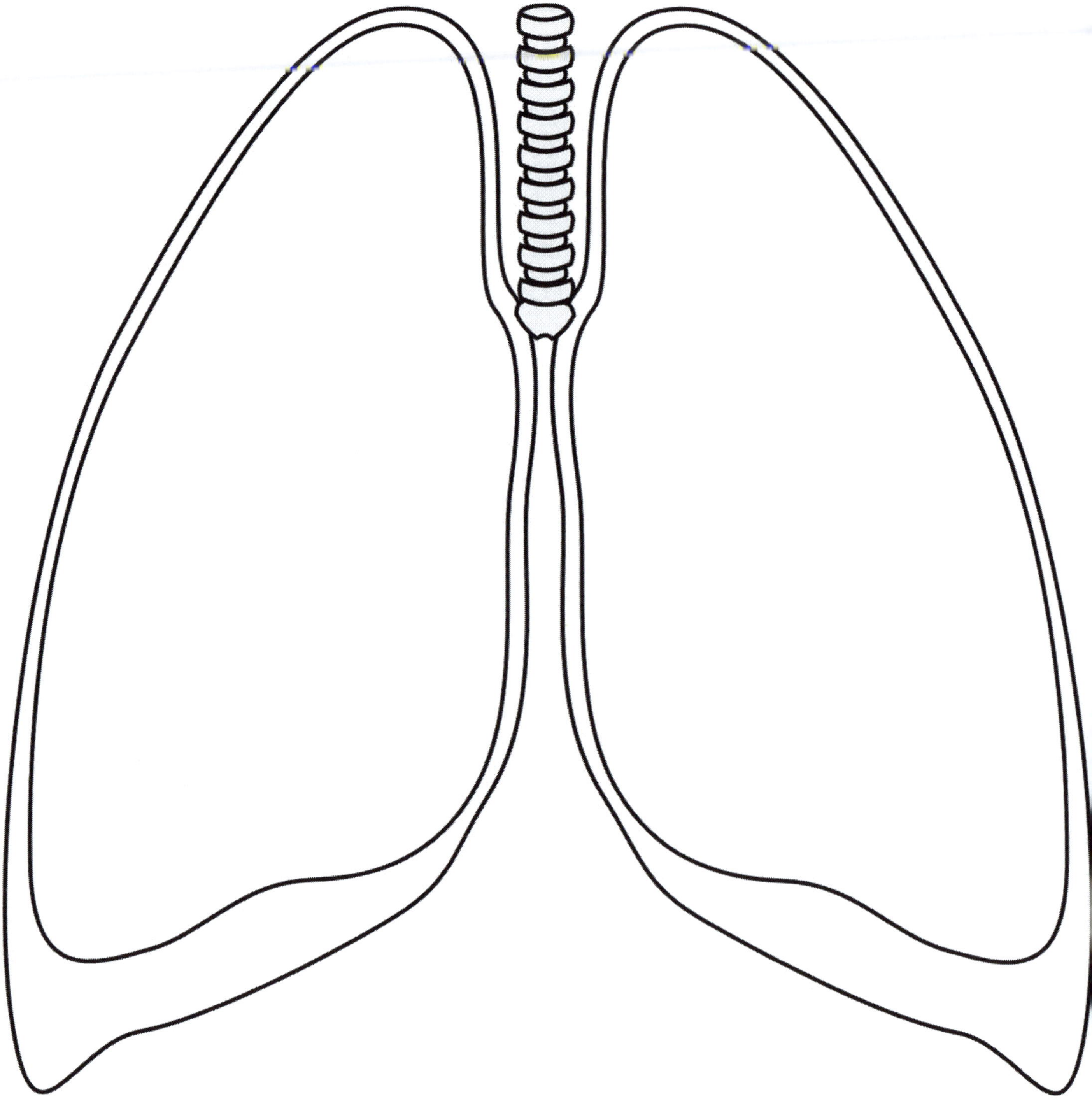

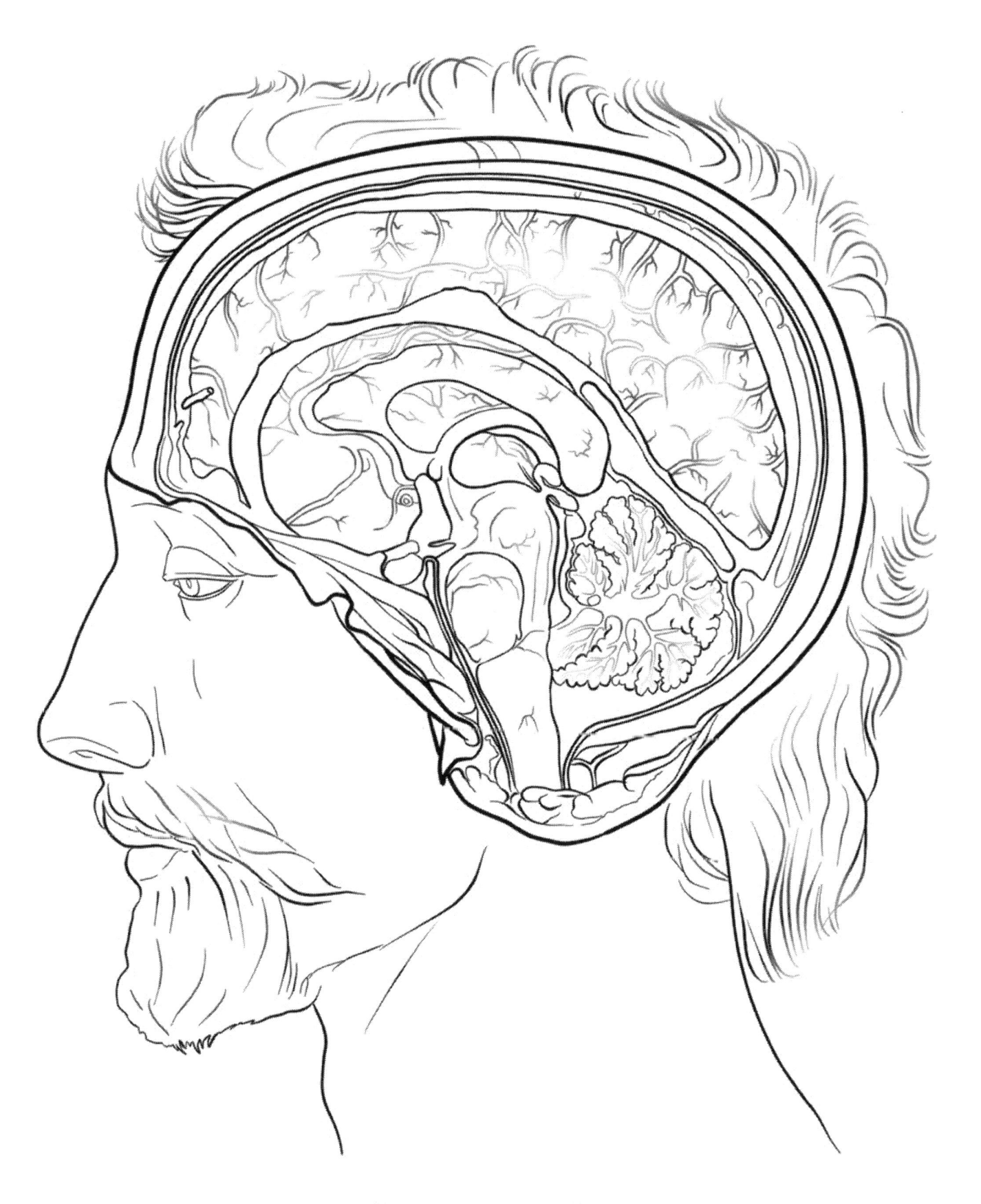

Human Brain

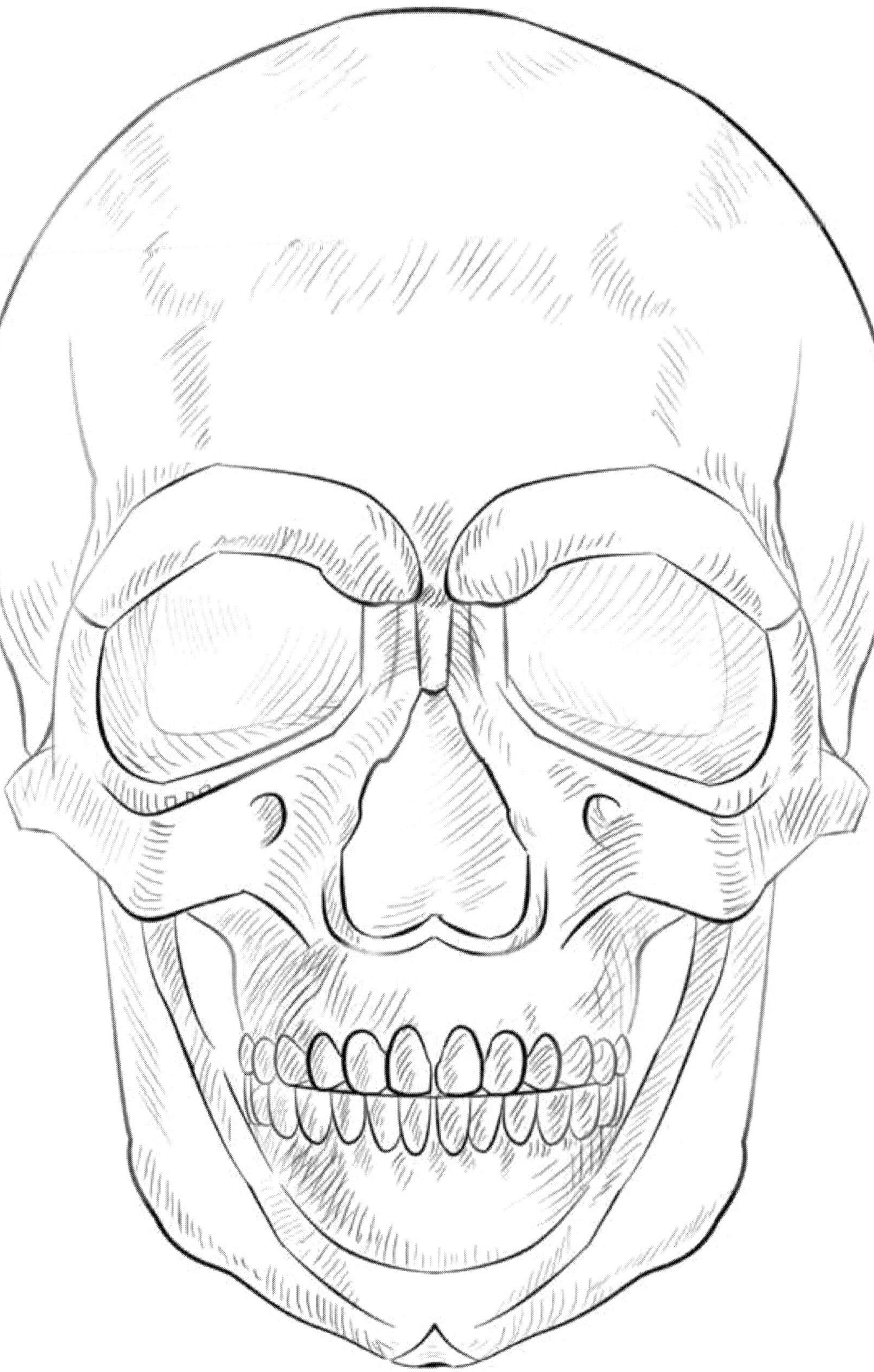

Central Nervous System

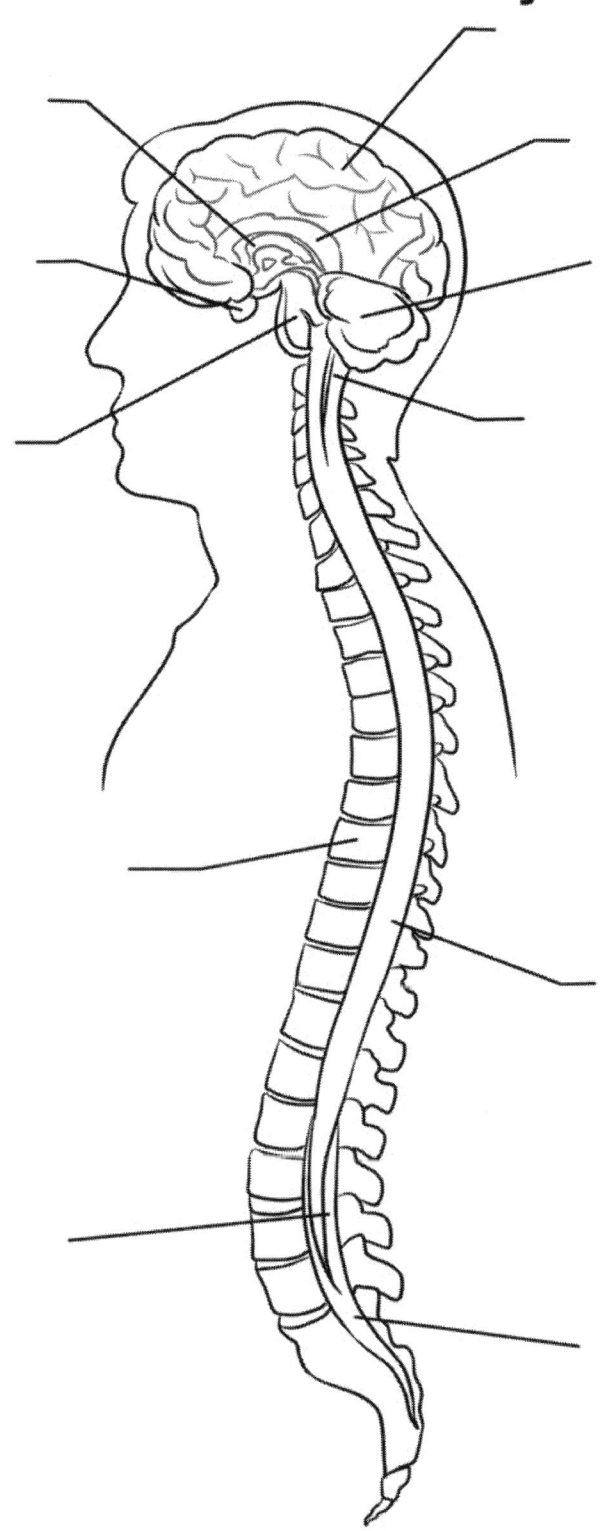

Word Bank

Body of Formix	Cerebellum	Callosum	Pons Varolii
Brain Stem	Cerebrum	Dura Mater	Spinal Cord
Cauda Equina	Corpus	Pituitary Gland	Vertebral Column

Human Circulatory System

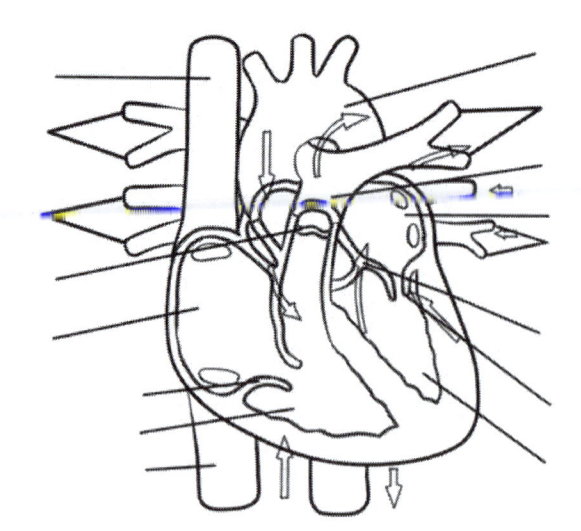

Word Bank
1. Aorta
2. Aortic semilunar valve
3. Interior vena cava
4. Left atrium
5. Left pulmonary arteries
6. Left pulmonary veins
7. Left ventricle
8. Mitral valve
9. Pulmonary semilunar valve
10. Pulmonary thunk
11. Right atrium
12. Riht pulmonary arteries
13. Riht pulmonry veins
14. Riht ventricle
15. Superior vena cava
16. Tricuspid valve

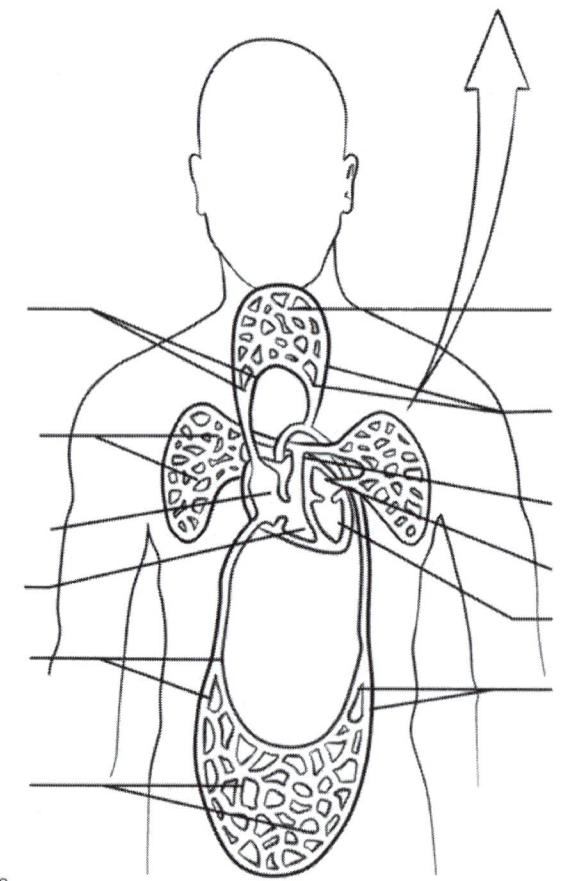

1. Left atrium
2. Left ventricle
3. Pulmonary capillaries in lungs
4. Pulmonary trunk
5. Right atrium
6. Right ventricle
7. Systemic capillaries of lower body
8. Systemic arteries to lower body
9. Systemic capillaries of upper body
10. Systemic veins from lower body
11. Systemic veins from upper body
12. Systemik arteries to upper body

Bones of the hand and wrist

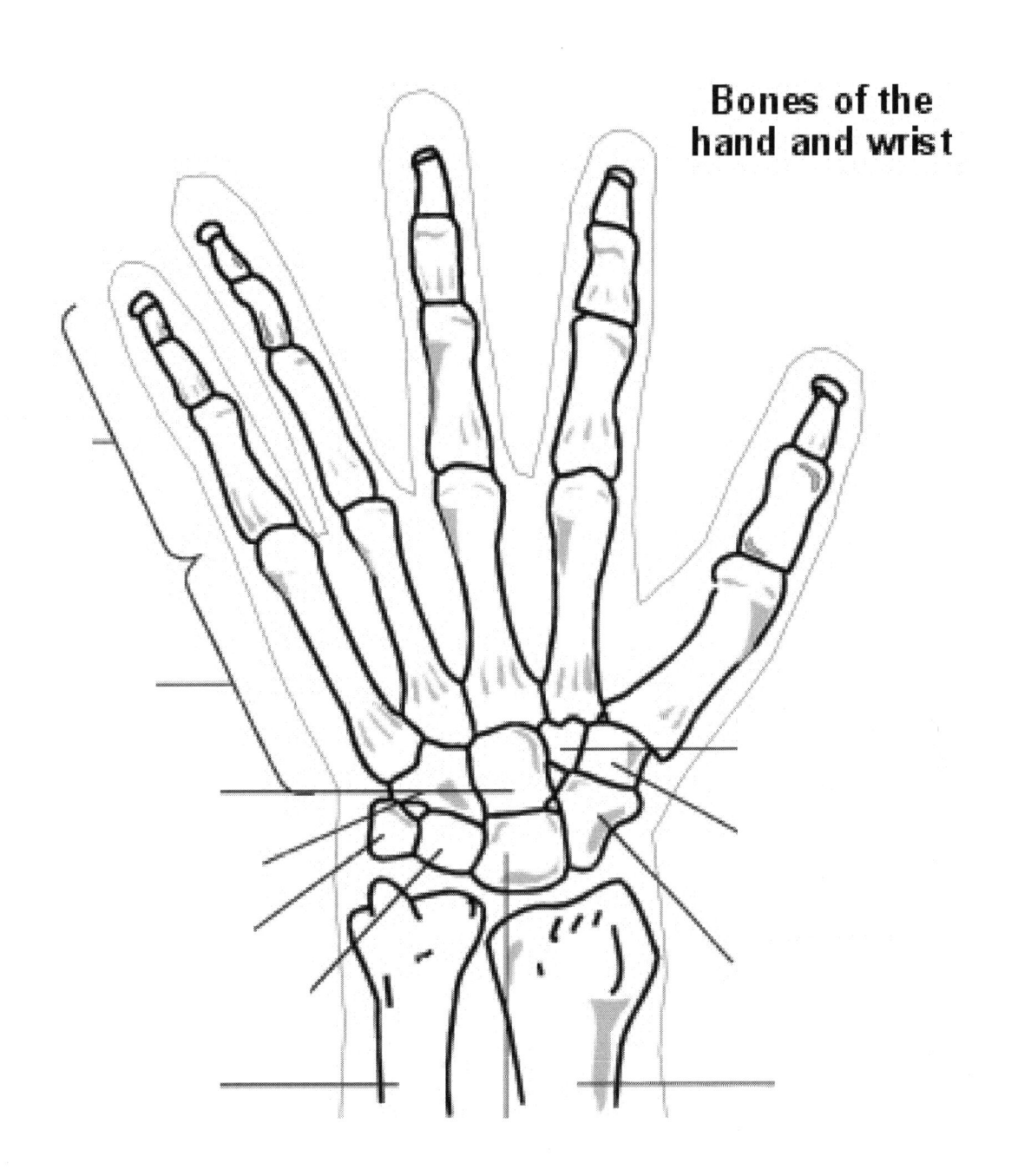

The Human Cell

Word Bank
1. Cell coat
2. Centriole
3. Chromatin
4. Cytoplasm
5. Free ribosome
6. Golgi body
7. Lysosome
8. Mitochondrion
9. Nuclear envelope
10. Nuclear pore
11. Nucleolus
12. Nucleus
13. Plasma membrane
14. Ribosome
15. Rough endoplasmic reticulum
16. Smooth endoplasmic reticulum

Lower Leg and Foot

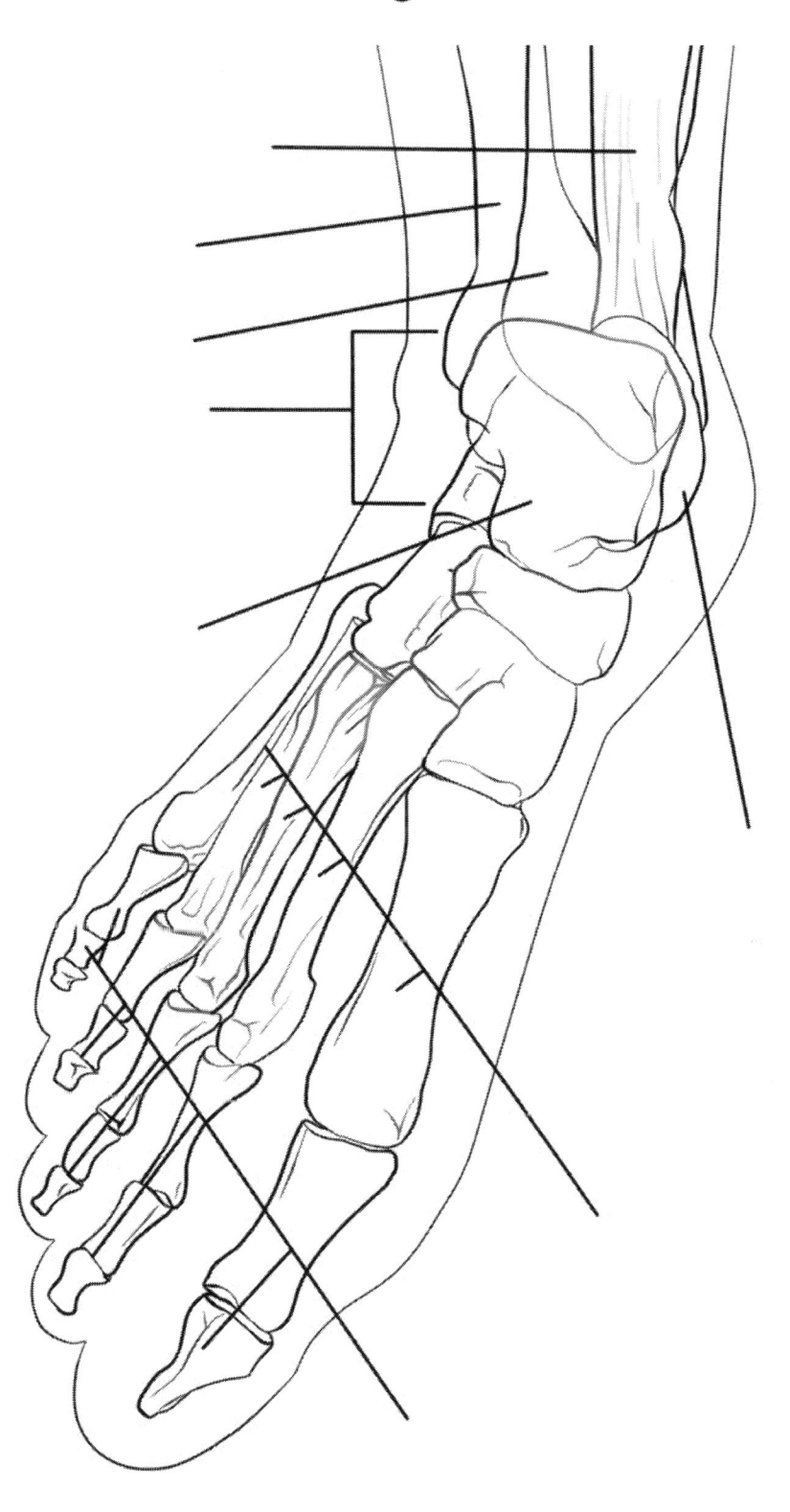

Word Bank

Tibia
Talus
Phalnges

Metatarsals
Fibula
Calcaneus

Ankle joint
Achilles tendon

The Components of the Digestive System

Word Bank
Stomach
Rectum
Pharynx
Liver
Jejunum
Duodenum
Descending colon
Cecum
Appendix
Anus

Anatomy of the Eye

Word Bank
Blood Vessels
Choroid
Cornea
Iris
Lens
Muscle
Optic Disc
Pupil
Retina
Sclera

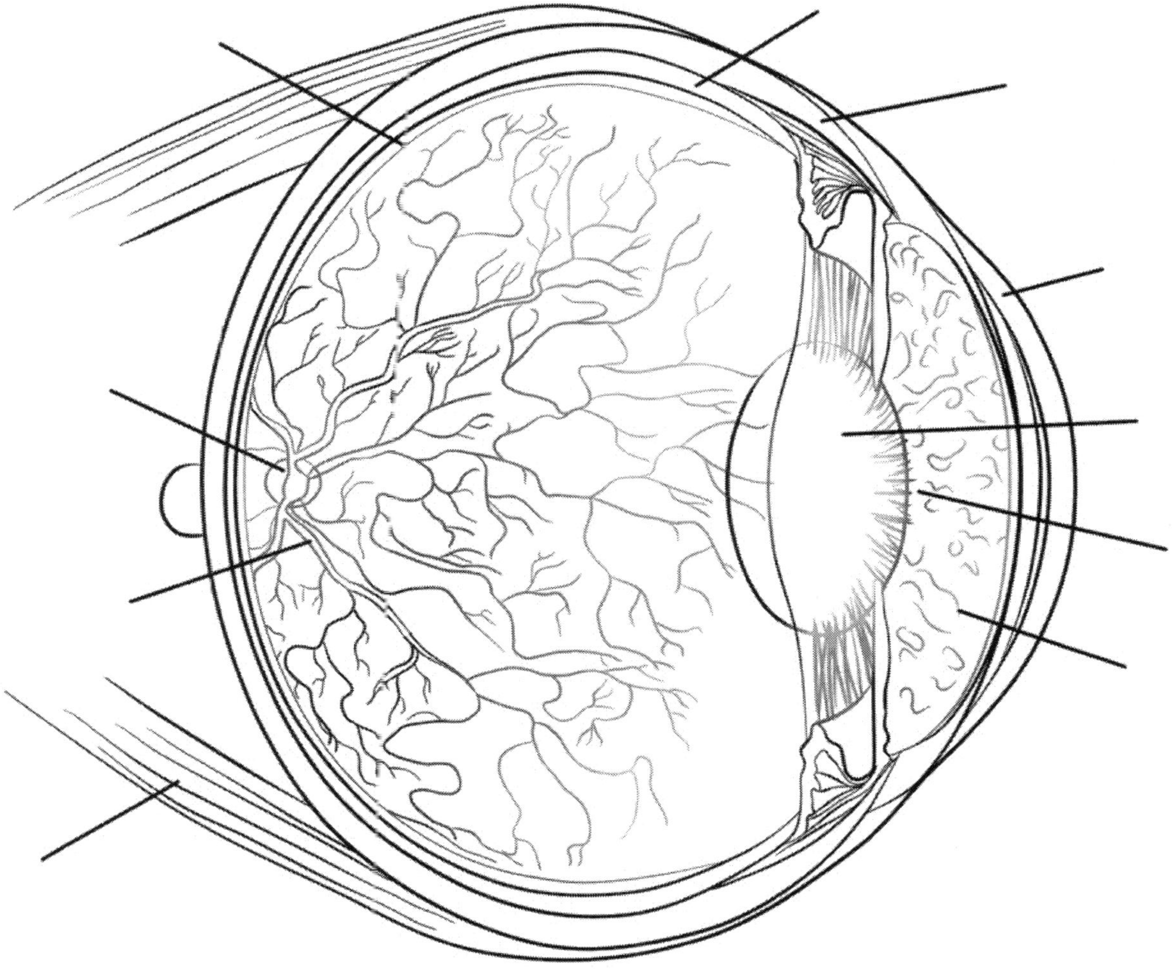

Word Bank
Apex of heart
Arch of aorta
Ascending aorta
Auricle of left atrium
Auricle of right atrium
Fat and vessels in anterior interventricular sulcus
Fat and vessels in coronary sulcus
Inferior vena cava
Left pulmonary artery
Left pulmonary veins
Pulmonary trunk
Superior vena cava

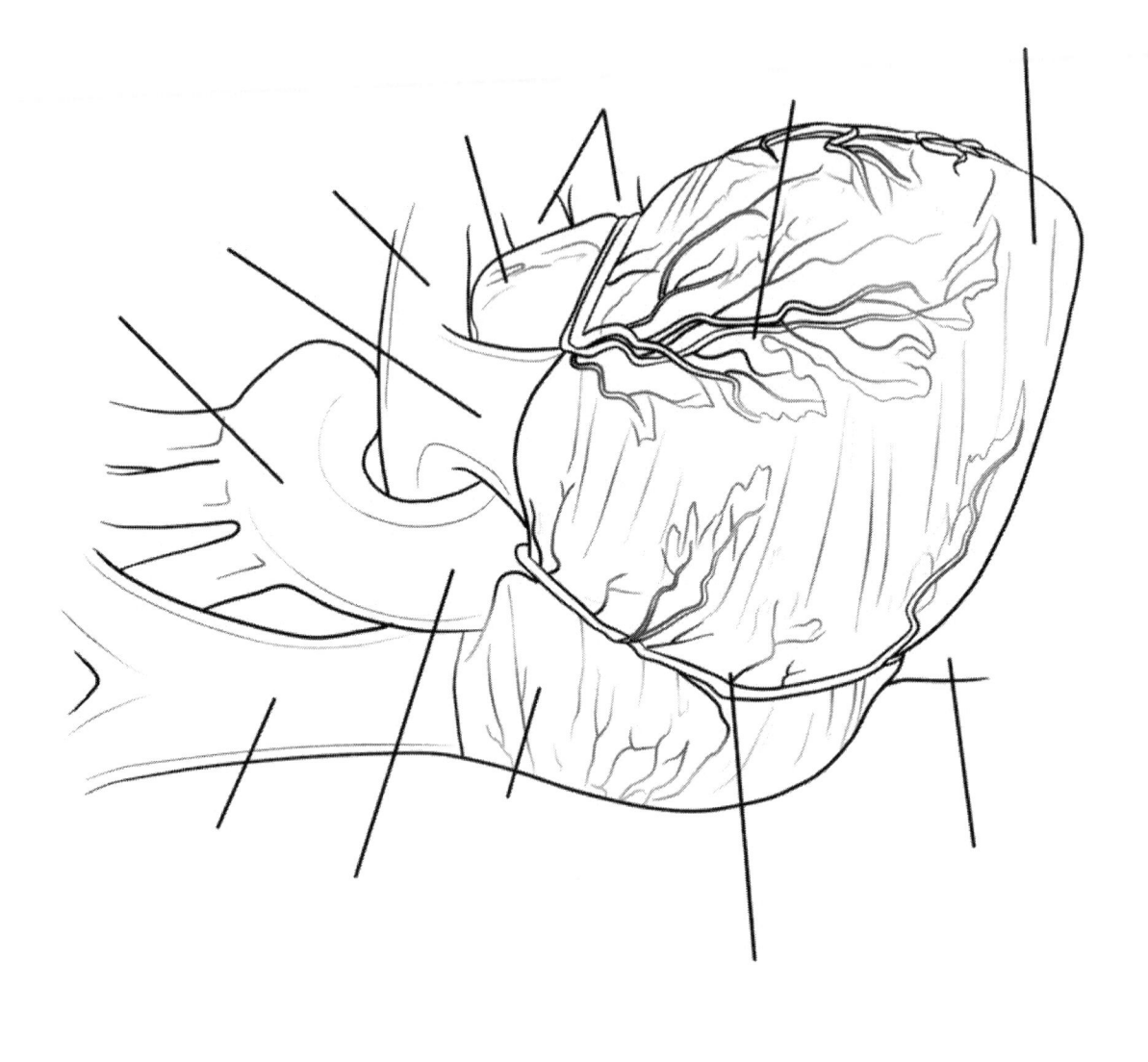

Superficial Heart Anatomy (Anterior)

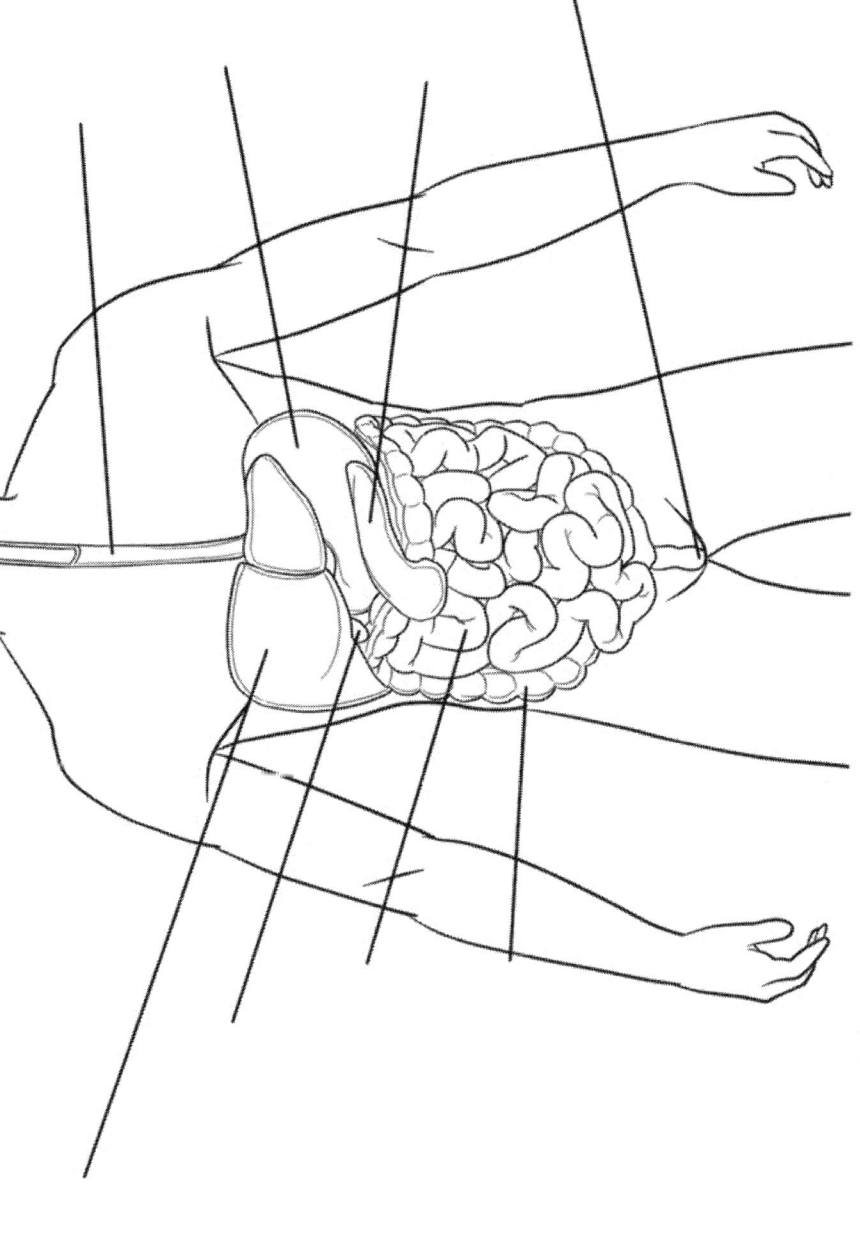

The Components of the Digestive System

Word Bank
- Stomach
- Small intestine
- Salivary glands
- Pharynx
- Pancreas
- Mouth
- Liver
- Large intestine
- Gallbladder
- Esophagus
- Anus

Human Brain

Word Bank
Basal Ganglia
Brain Stem
Cerebellum
Corex
Cranium
Dura
Frontal Lobe
Occipital Lobe
Parietal Lobe
Spinal Cord
Temporal Lobe

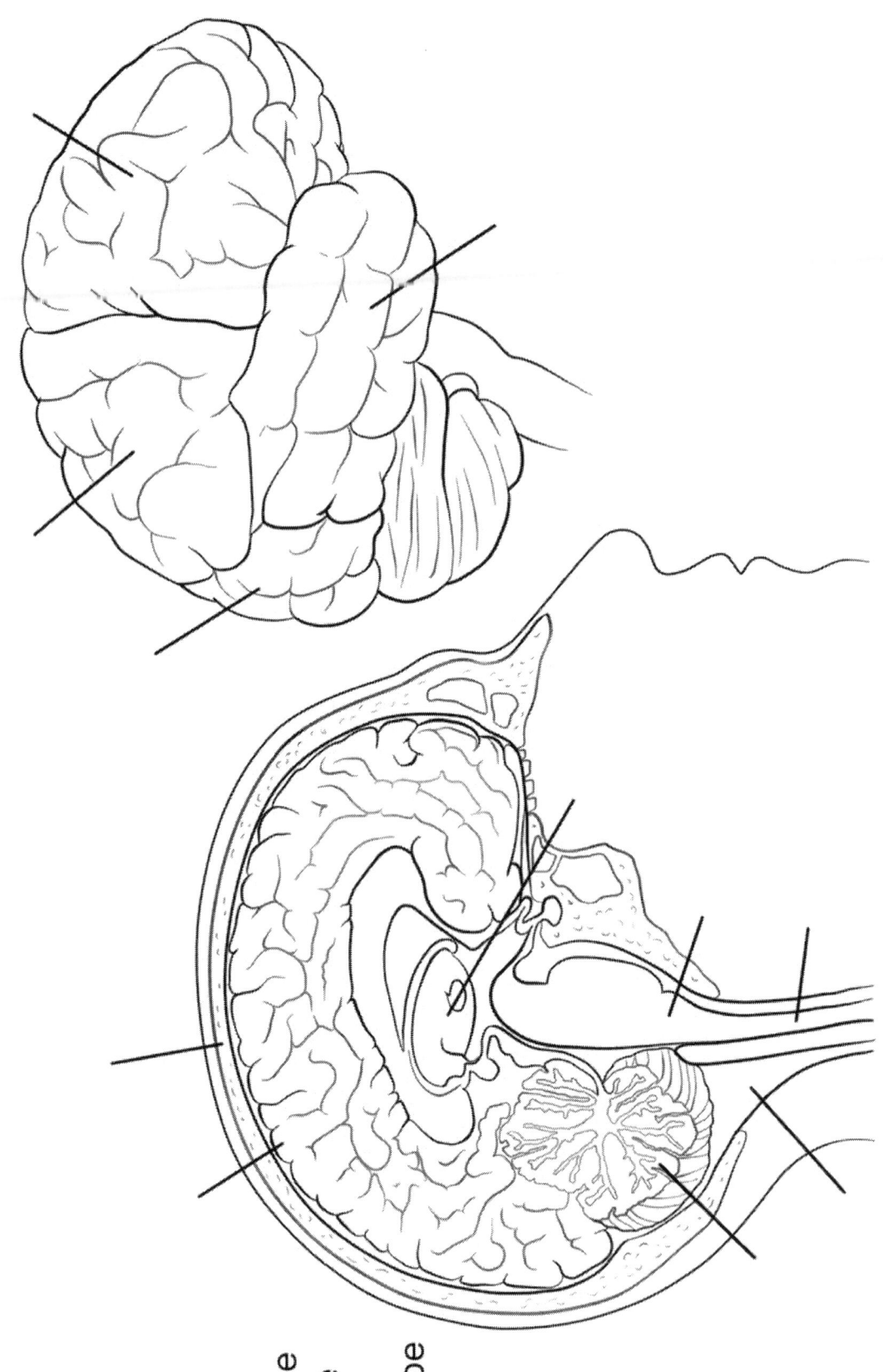

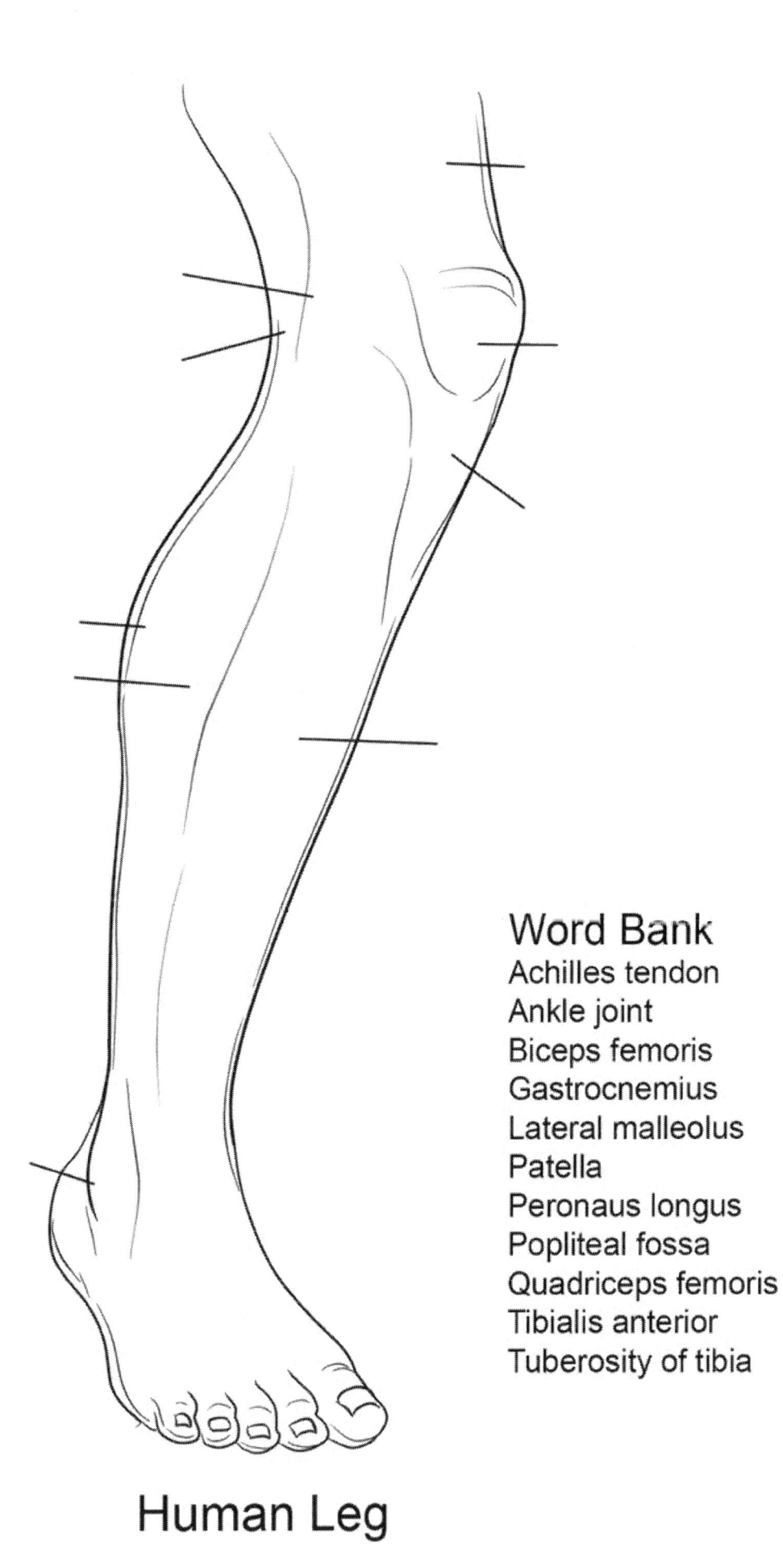

Human Leg

Word Bank
Achilles tendon
Ankle joint
Biceps femoris
Gastrocnemius
Lateral malleolus
Patella
Peronaus longus
Popliteal fossa
Quadriceps femoris
Tibialis anterior
Tuberosity of tibia

Human Leg

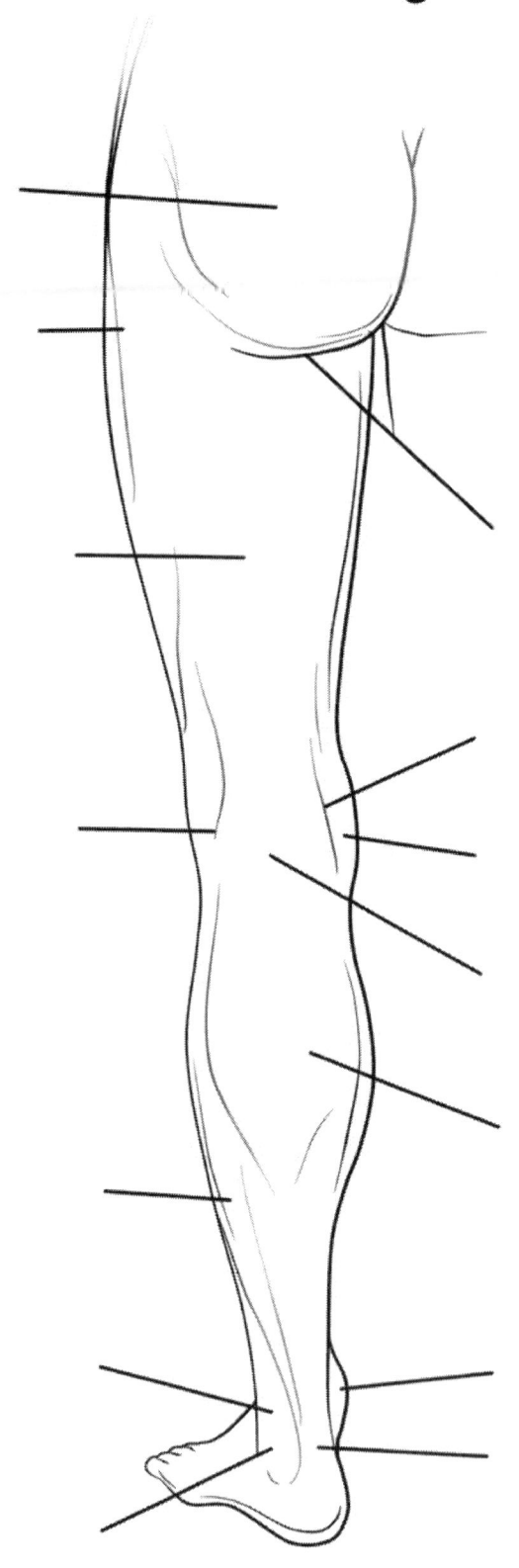

Word Bank

Biceps femoris	Hamstrings	Popliteal fossa	Tensor fasciae latae
Gastrocnemius	Lateral malleolus	Semimembranosus	Perona longus an
Gluteal fold	Medial malleolus	Semitendinosus	brevis
Gluteus maximus	Tendo calcneus	Soleus	

Word Bank

Cardiac notch
Inferior lobe
Left lung
Lobar (secondary) bronchus
Main (primary) bronchus
Middle lobe
Right lung
Segmental (tertiary) bronchus
Superior lobe
Superior lobe
Trachea

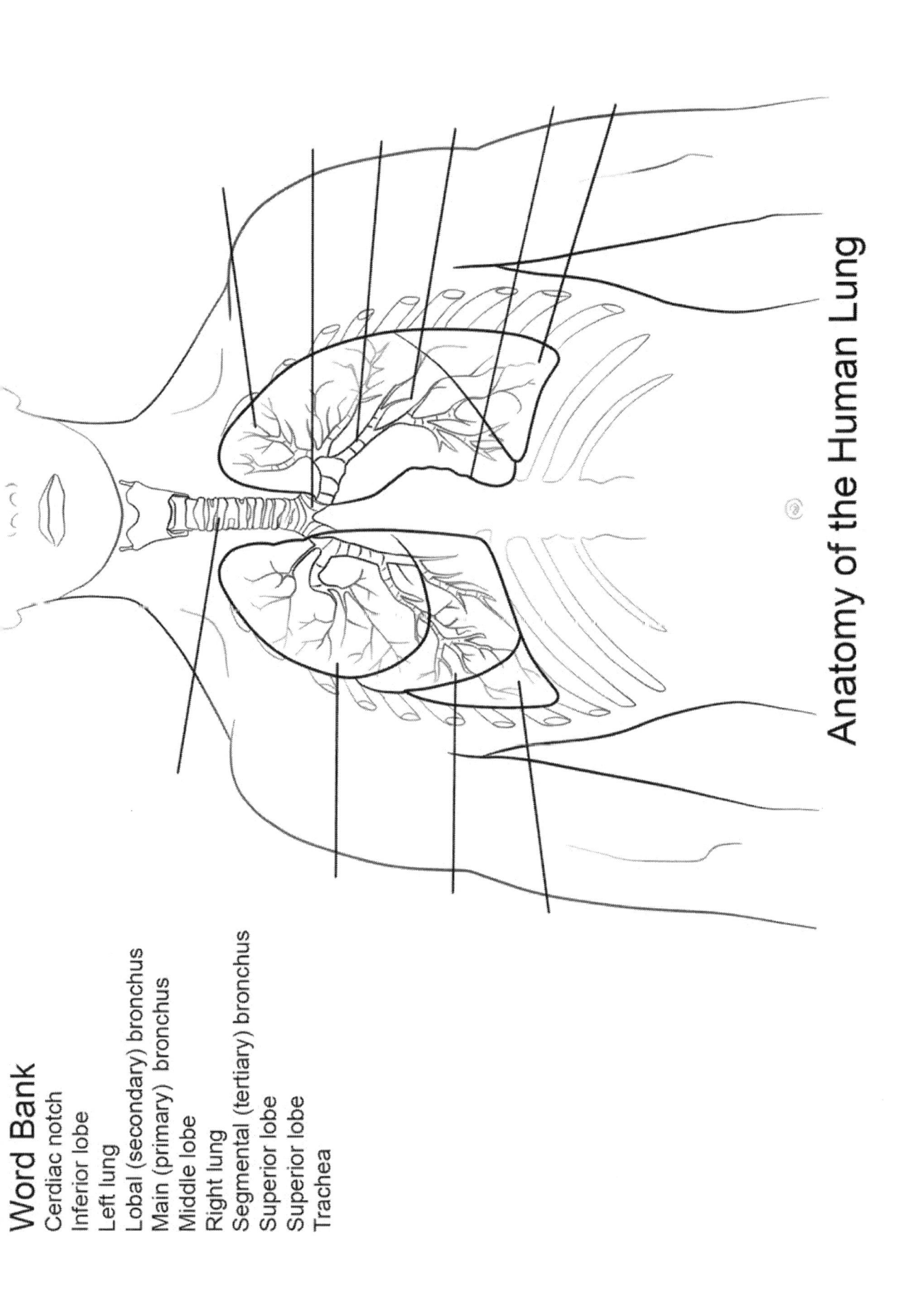

Anatomy of the Human Lung

Human Muscles

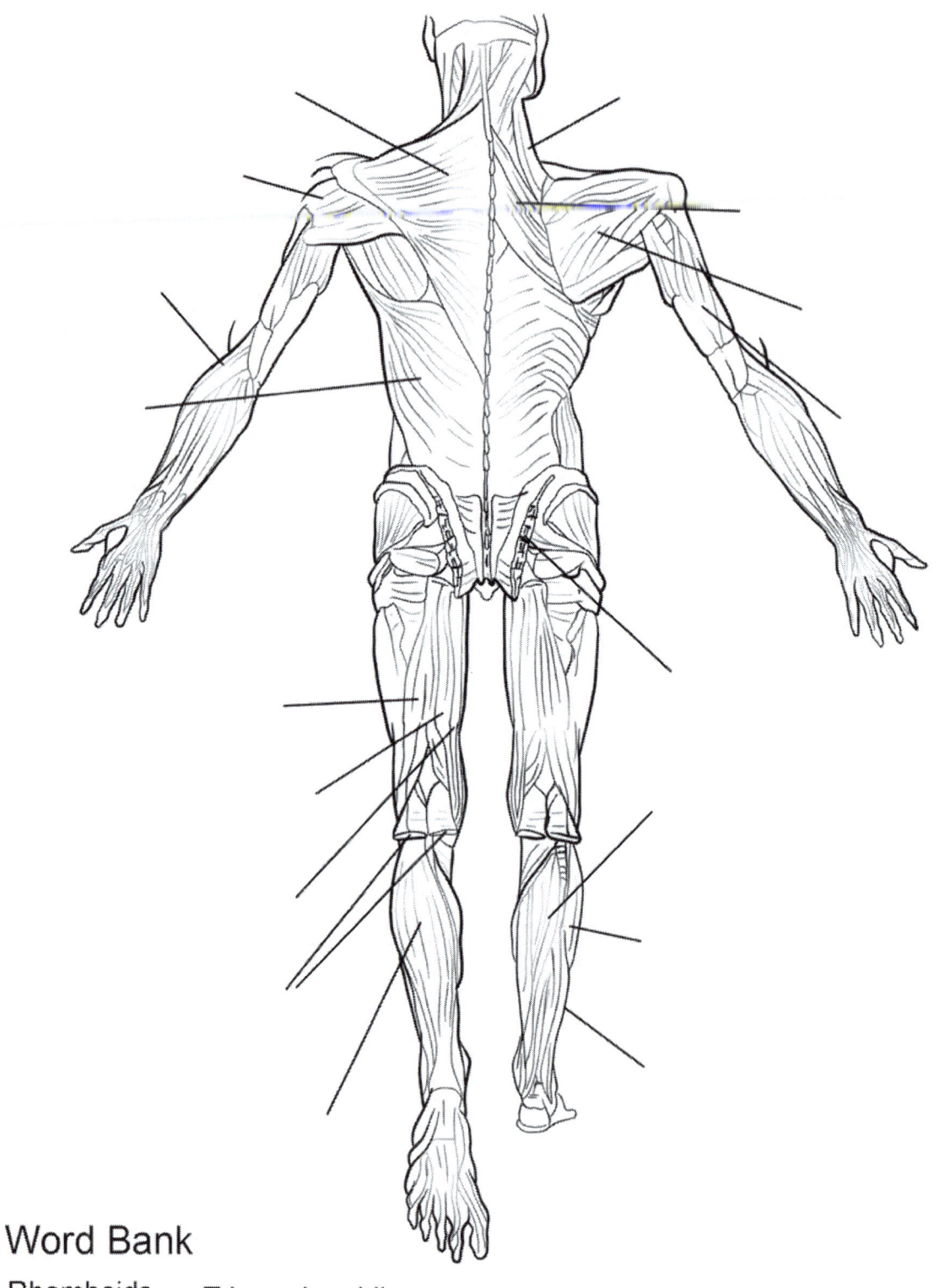

Word Bank

Rhomboids
Trapezius
Deltoid
Soleus
Rotator cuff

Triceps brachii
Biceps femoris
Brachioradialis
Gastrocnemius
Latissimus dorsi

Levator scapulae
Peroneus brevis
Peroneus longus
Semimembranosus
Semitendinosus

Tibialis posterior
Gluteus maximus

Human Muscles

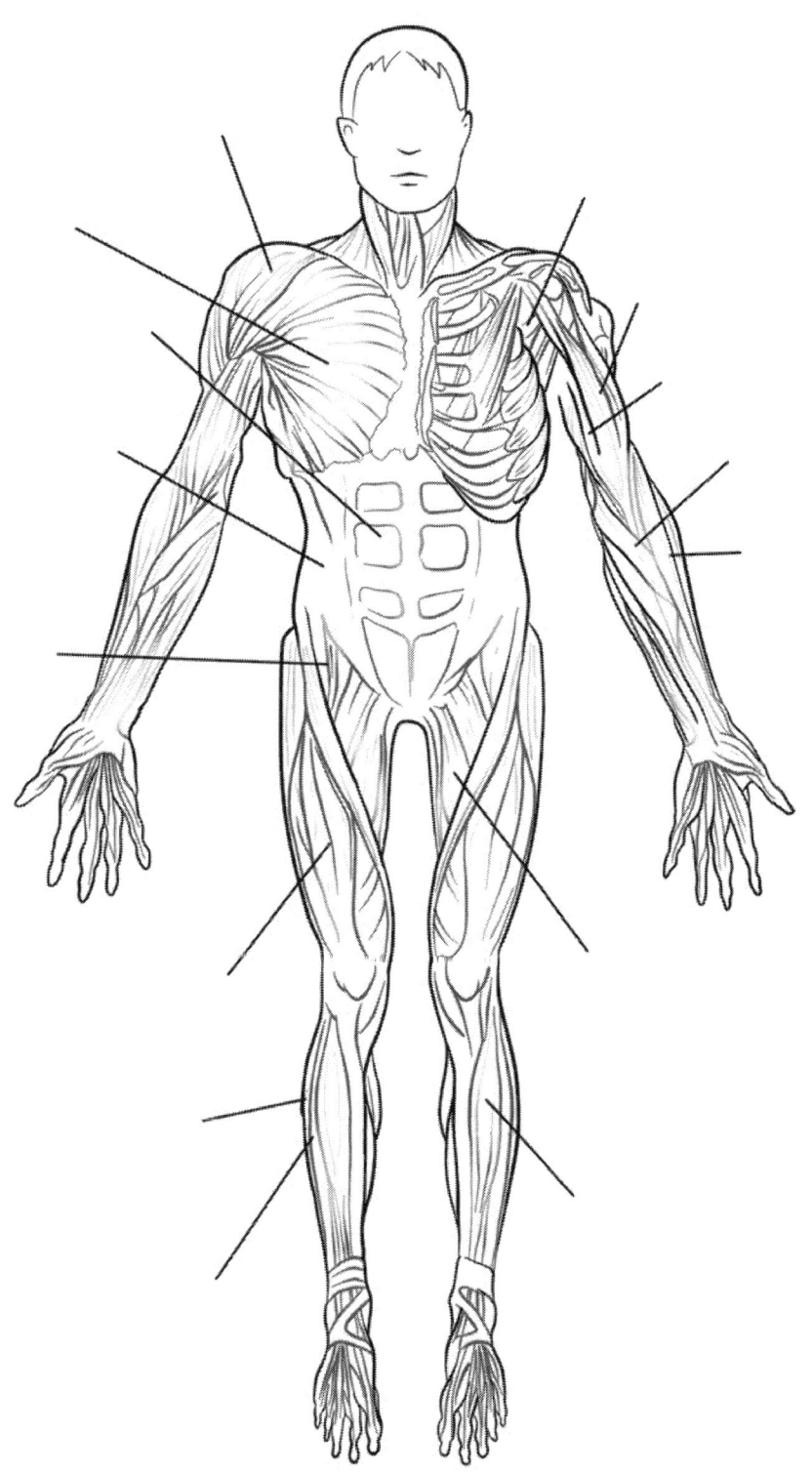

Word Bank

Brachialis
Deltoid
Iliopsoas
Biceps brachii

Pectoralis major
Peroneus brevis
Peroneus longus
Pronator teres

Rectus abdominis
Rotator cuff
Tibialis anterior
Brachioradialis

Abdominal external oblique
Quadriceps femoris
Adductor muscles

Human Skeletal System

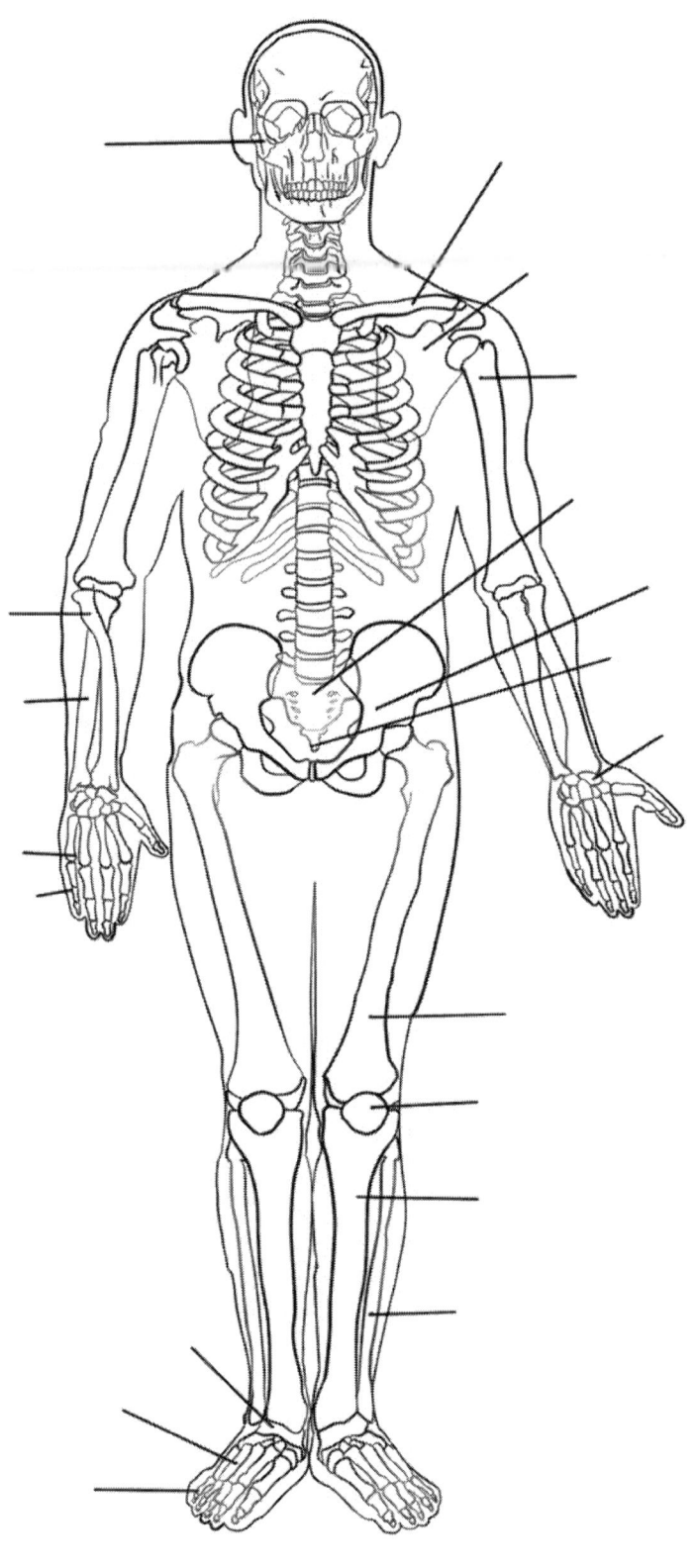

Word Bank

Ulna	Patella	Humerus	Carpal bones
Tibia	Scapula	Hip bone	Auditory ossicles
Fibula	Sacrum	Phalanges	Metatarsal bones
Femur	Coccyx	Phalanges	Metacarpal bones
Radius	Clavicle	Tarsal bones	

Human Skeleton

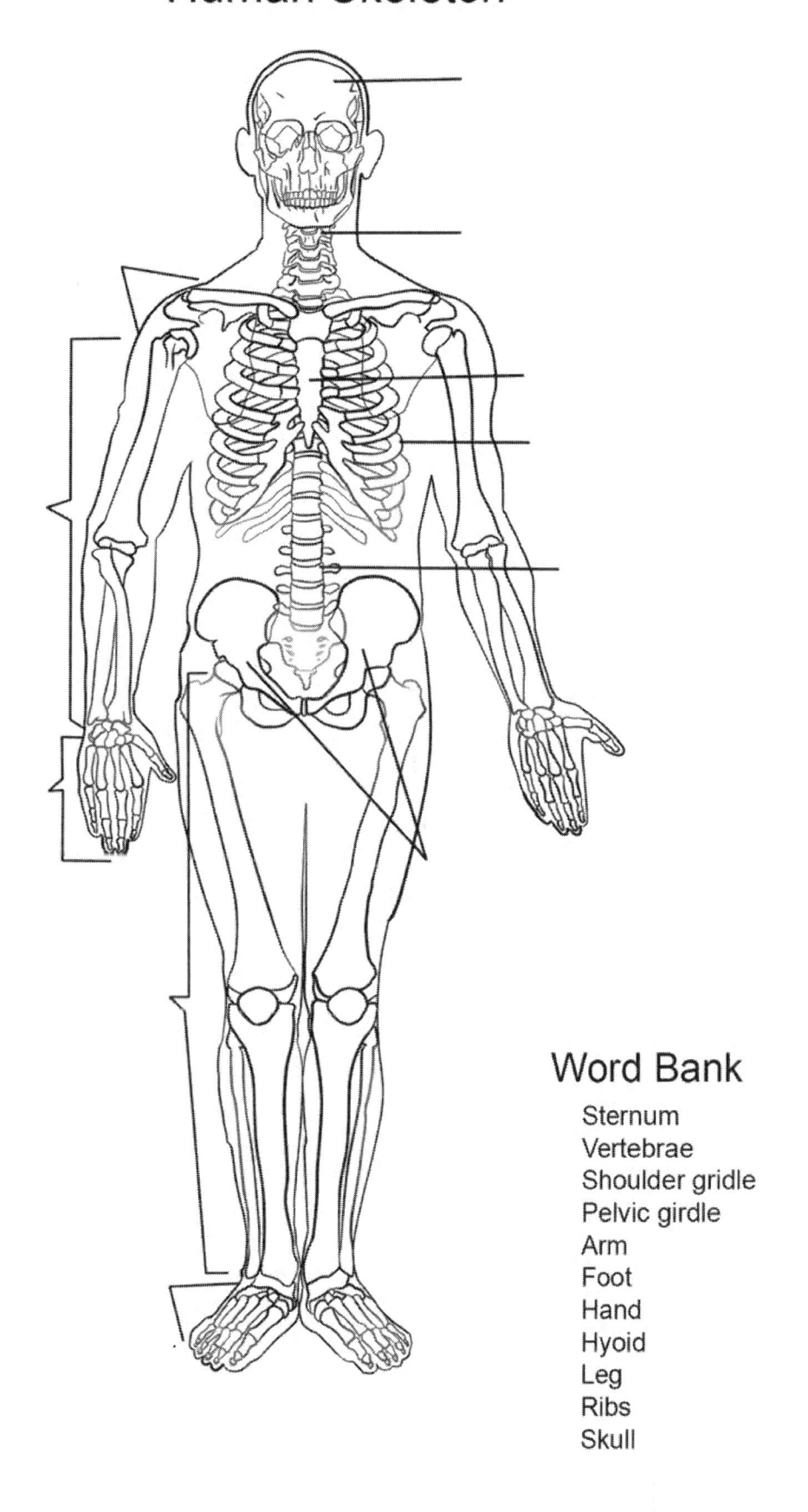

Word Bank
Sternum
Vertebrae
Shoulder gridle
Pelvic girdle
Arm
Foot
Hand
Hyoid
Leg
Ribs
Skull

The Human Skin

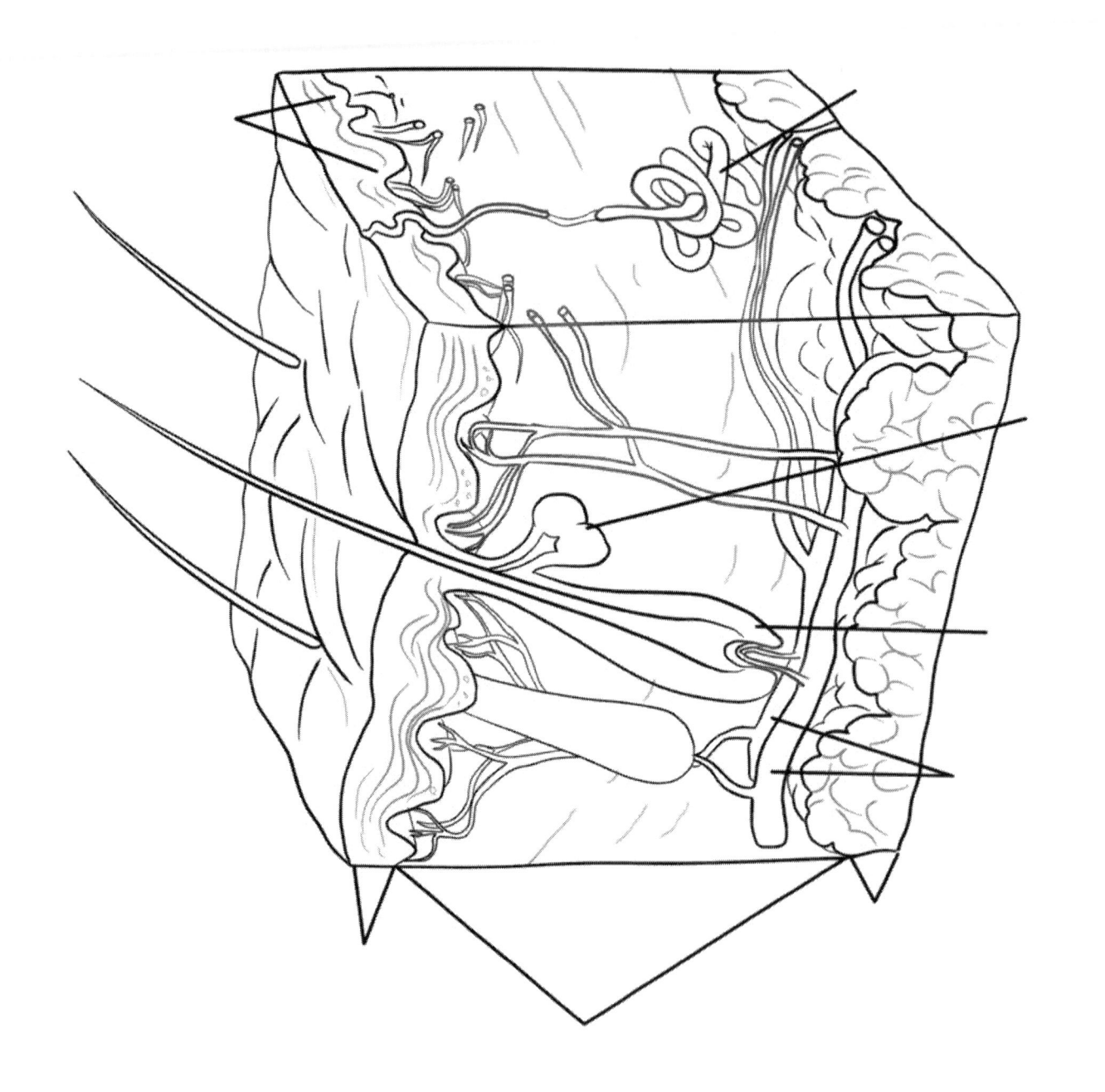

Word Bank

1. Pyloric canal
2. Body
3. Fundus
4. Angular incisure
5. Pyloric antrum
6. Pylorus
7. Duodenum
8. Cardia
9. Esophagus
10. Cardial noth

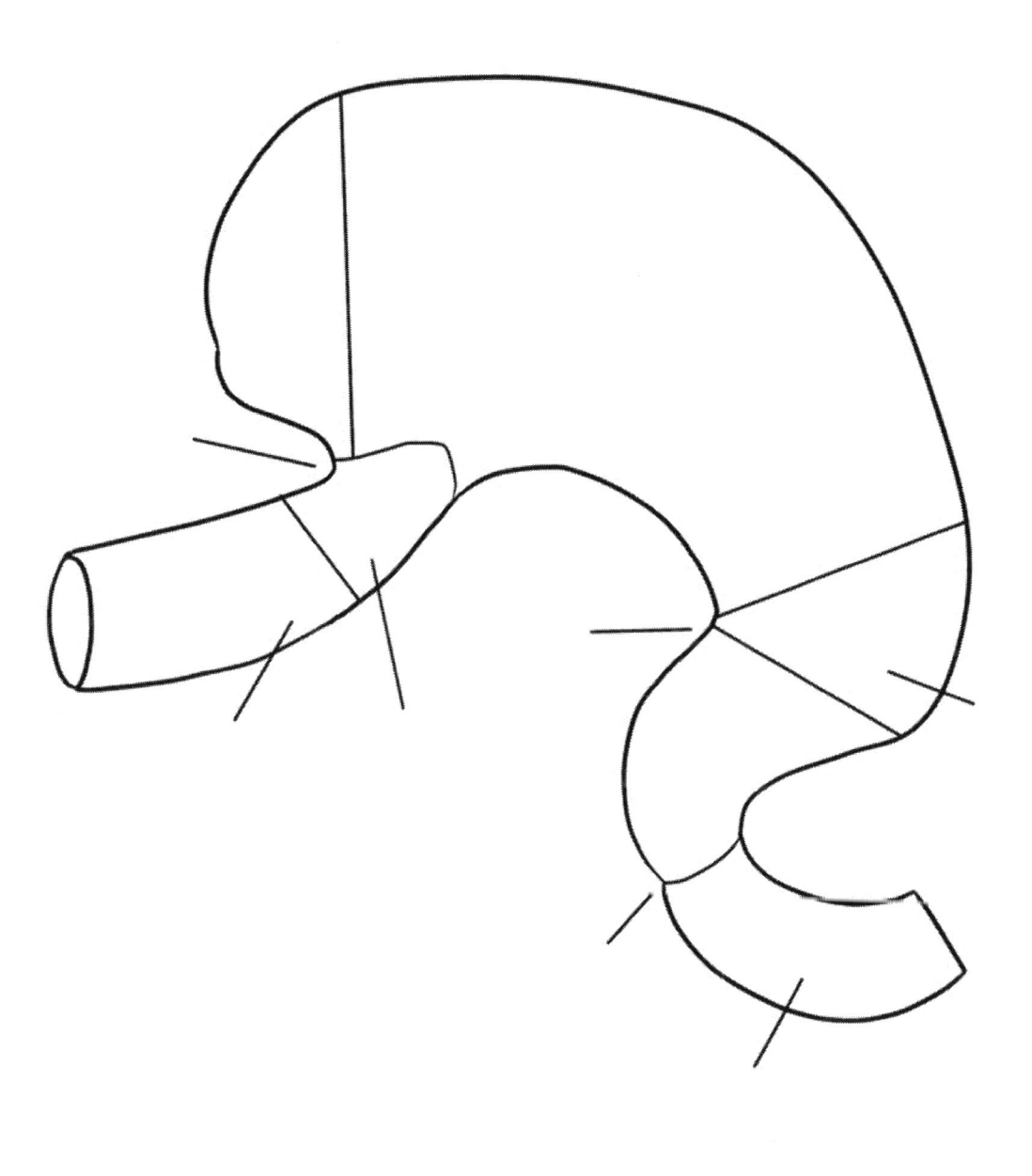

Human Stomach

Human Immune System

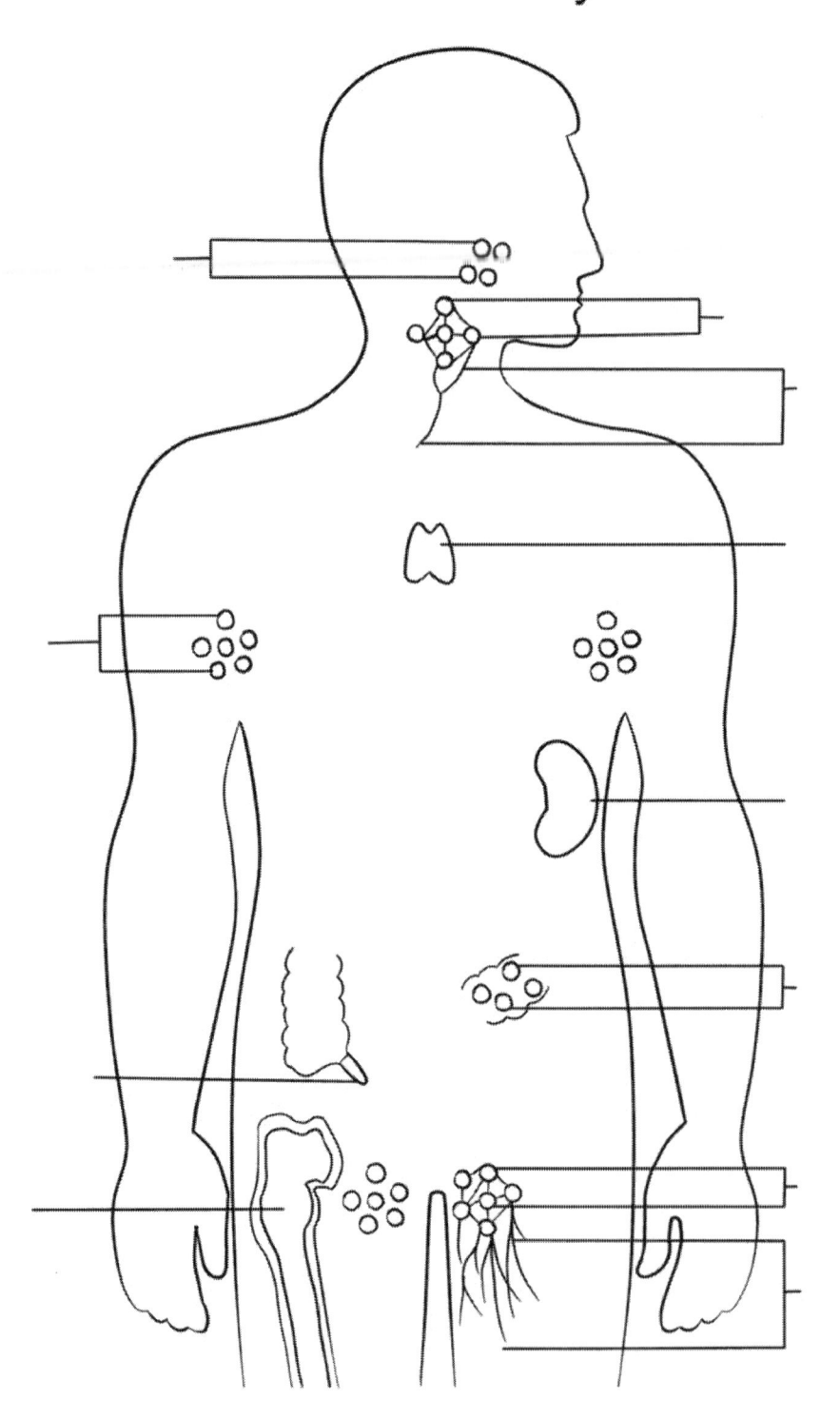

Word Bank

Appendix
Spleen
Thymus
Bone marrow
Lymph nodes
Lymph nodes
Lymph nodes
Lymphatic vessels
Lymphatic vessels
Peyer's patches
Tonsils and adenoids

Word Bank

1. Vas deferens
2. Urethral opening
3. Testis
4. Suspensory ligament of penis
5. Sigmoid colon
6. Seminal vesicle
7. Scrotum
8. Rectum
9. Puboprostatic ligament
10. Pubic bone
11. Prostate gland
12. Perineal membrane
13. Penis
14. Glands penis
15. Foreskin
16. External uretral sphincter
17. Epididymis
18. Ejaculatory duct
19. Cowper's gland
20. Corpus cavernosum
21. Bladder
22. Anus

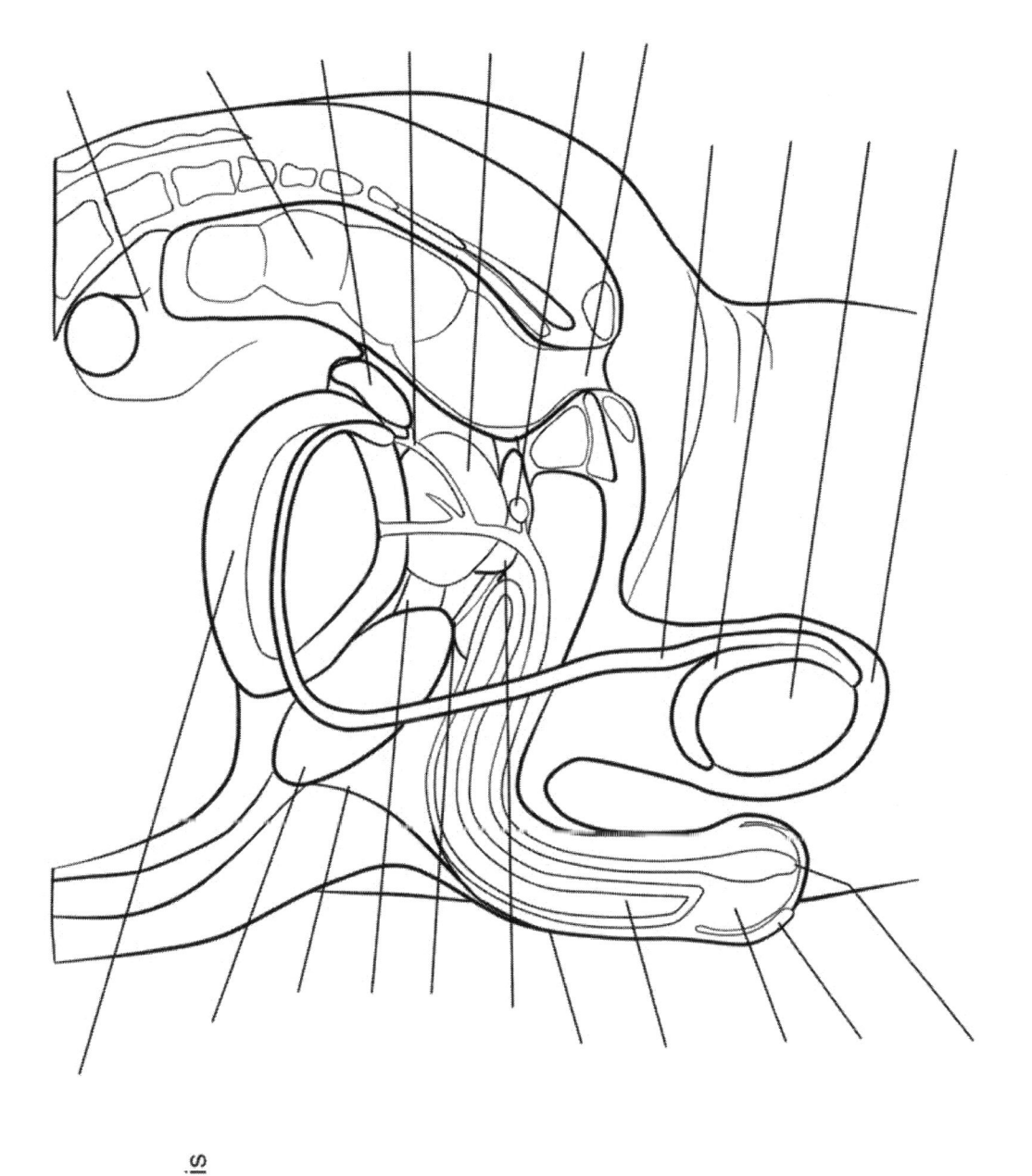

Male reproductive system

Human Lymphatic System

Word Bank
Adenoid
Bllod capillary
Bone marrow
Interstitial fluid
Lymph node
Lymph nodes
Lymph vessel
Lymphatic capillary
Lymphatic vessel
Spleen
Thymus
Tissue cell
Tonsil
Masses of lymphocytes and macrophages
Right lymphatic duct, entering vein

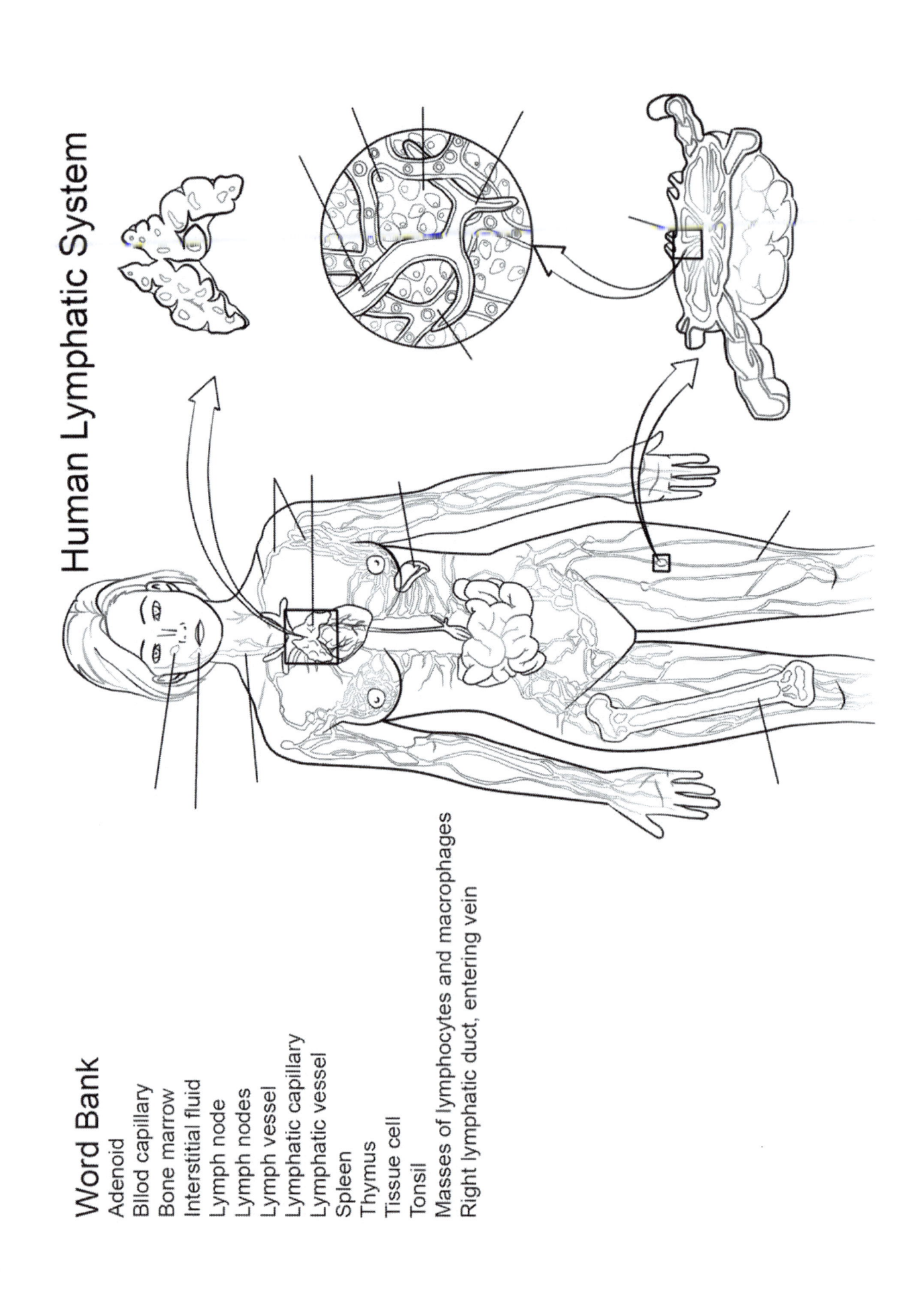

The Respiratory System

Word Bank
Alveoli
Bronchioles
Bronchus
Diaphragm
Frontal sinus
Larynx
Left lung
Nasal cavity
Nasal conchae
Nose
Pharynx
Right lung
Sphenoidal sinus
Trachea

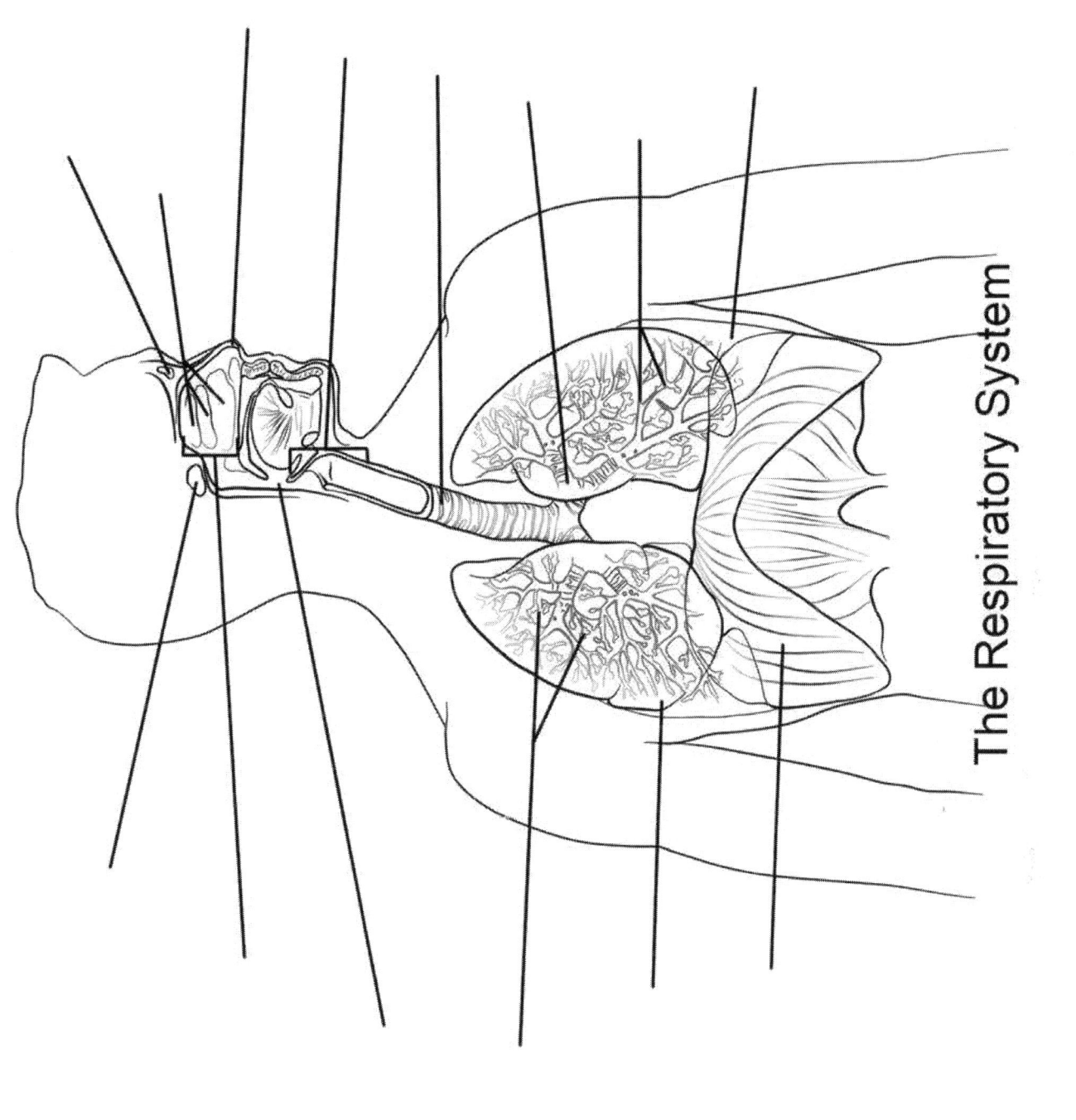

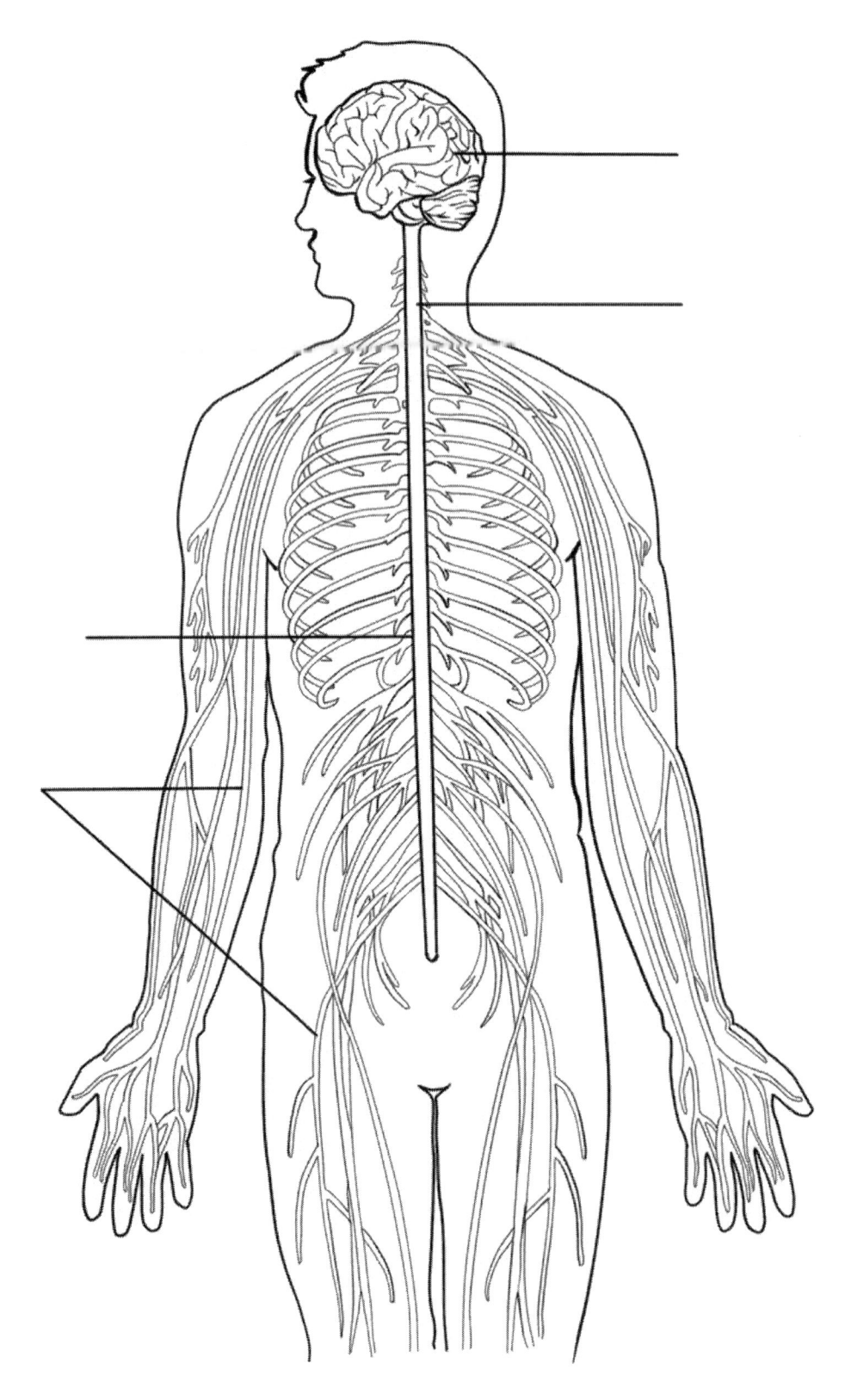

Word Bank

Brain	Nerve	Peripheral Nervous System
Ganglion	Spinal cord	Central Nervous System

The Urinary System

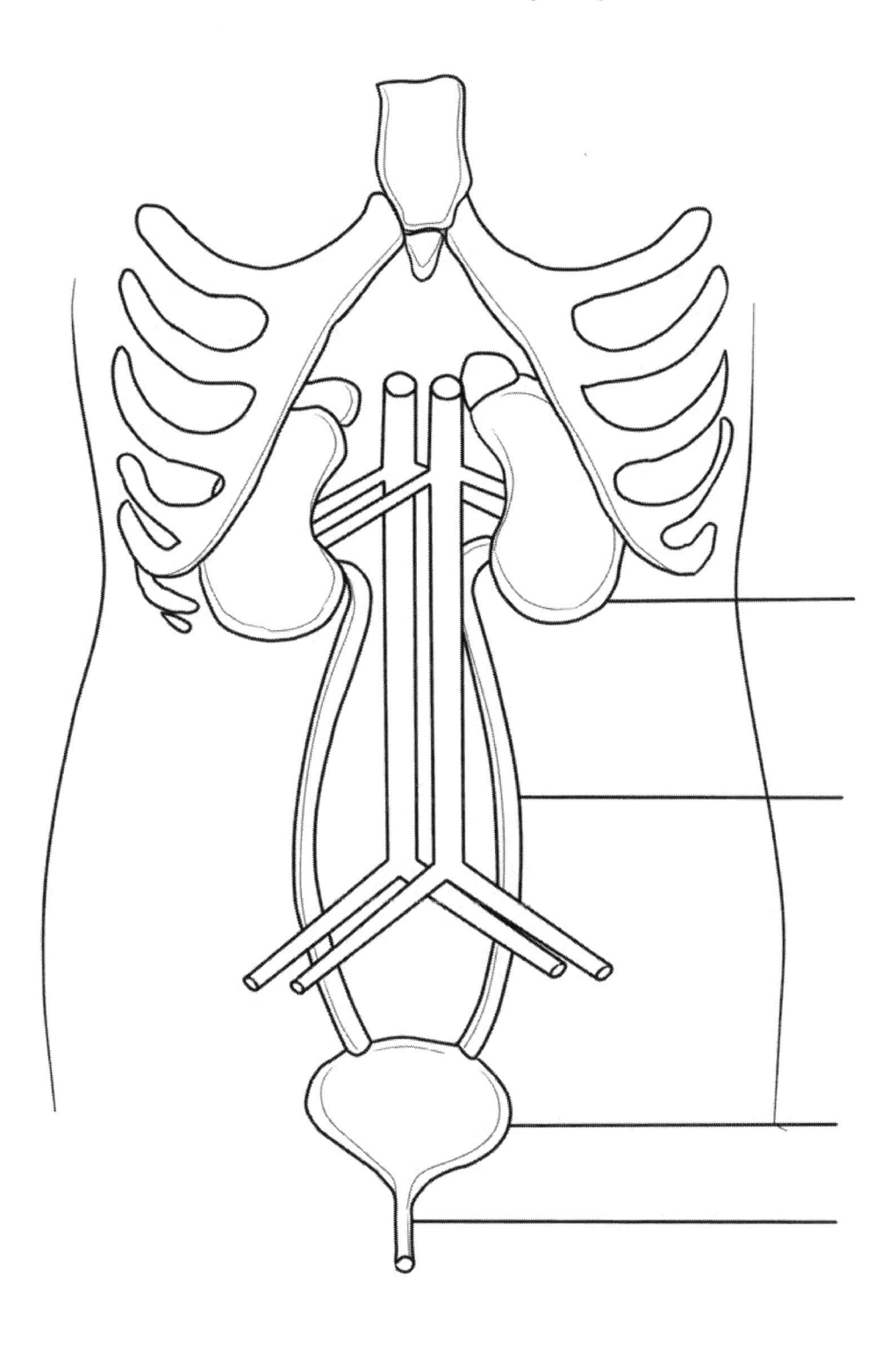

Word Bank
Bladder   Kidney   Ureter   Urethra

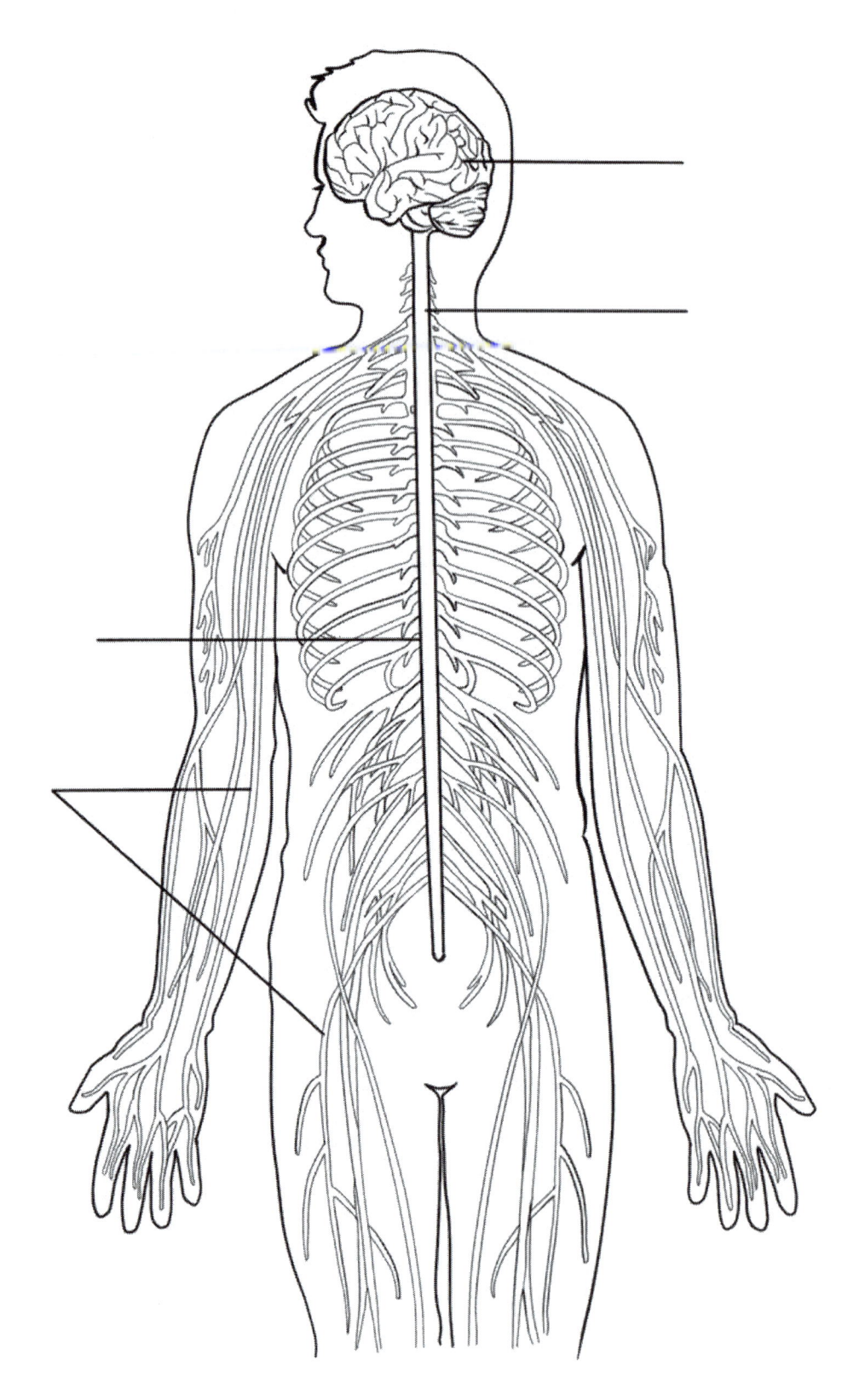

Word Bank

Brain	Nerve	Peripheral Nervous System
Ganglion	Spinal cord	Central Nervous System

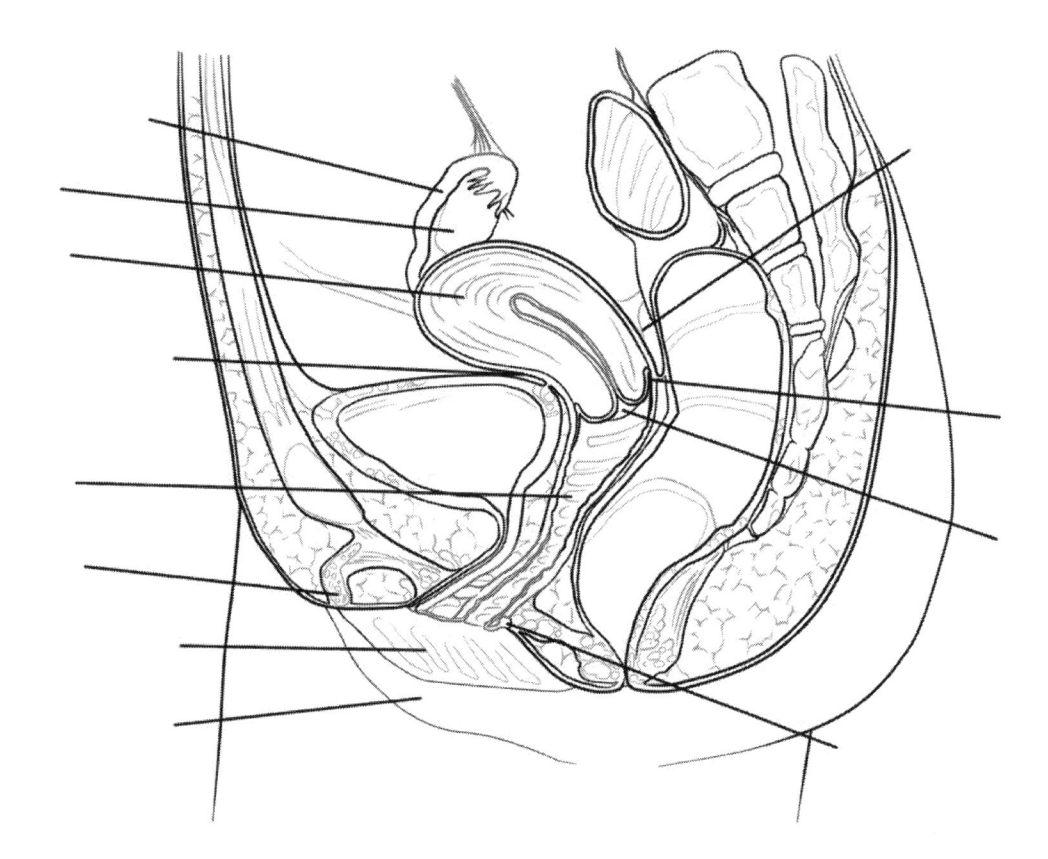

Word Bank
Cervix
Clitorus
Formix
Greater vestibular gland
Labium majus
Labium minus
Ovary
Rectouterine pouch
Uterine tube
Uterus
Vagina
Vesicouterine pouch

The Female Reproductive System

Printed in Great Britain
by Amazon